REMINISCENCES

OF

AN OLD GEORGIA LAWYER.

BY

GARNETT ANDREWS,
JUDGE OF THE SUPERIOR COURTS OF GEORGIA.

Cherokee Publishing Company
Atlanta, Georgia

1984

Library of Congress Cataloging in Publication Data

Andrews, Garnett, 1798-1873.
  Reminiscences of an old Georgia lawyer.

  Reprint. Originally published: Atlanta, Ga.
Franklin Steam Print. House, 1870. With new introd.
  1. Andrews, Garnett, 1798-1873. 2. Judges--
Georgia--Biography. I. Title.
KF368.A48A37   1984   349.759'092'a [B] 84-12652
ISBN 0-87797-078-5   347.5900924 [B]

Introduction Copyright © 1984 by Robert M. Willingham, Jr.

All rights reserved. No part may be reproduced or transmitted in any form, by any means, electronic or mechanical, including photocopying and recording, or by any storage or retrieval system, without the permission in writing from the publisher.

Manufactured in the United States of America

ISBN: 978-0-87797-078-1 Hardcover
ISBN: 978-0-87797-326-3 Trade Paper

Cherokee Publishing Company is an operating division of The Larlin Corporation, P. O. Box 1730, Marietta, GA 30061.

INTRODUCTION

Piedmont Georgia in the early decades of the nineteenth century contained a rag-tag assortment of rambunctious rapscallions whose colorful ways and attitudes enlivened an existence generally mundane and difficult. These antebellum years saw the emergence of a staunch aristocracy based on cotton and slavery, but they also witnessed the struggles of the small farmer, non-subsistent, scuffling, often haggard, but never humorless.

Garnett Andrews's *Reminiscences of an Old Georgia Lawyer* captures not only the humor and vibrancy of this period, but also the poignancy and reality. Its rollicking style is filled with the local color of Georgia which provides character studies of the "real folk" of the time. These are not figures of fiction, but actual acquaintances of Judge Andrews - from the legendary wit John Mitchell Dooly to William H. Crawford, Tom Cobb, and Judge Clayton, from old Peter Bennett, "a high Jack Straw of an old fellow, that didn't care a damn," to "fat, square, and forty" Miss Nancy Rumsey. There are careful renditions of middle Georgia dialect, white and black. There are descriptions of customs like corn shuckings and "tavernizing," scenes from the mountains of Rabun and the plantations of Wilkes and the gold hunting of Dahlonega. The *Reminiscences* are rambling, but they also are skillfully done, by a man who had interest and compassion in people and to whom the law meant little except in its relationship to human beings.

Andrews was born in Wilkes County, Georgia, on 30 October 1798, and was the only one of the sixteen children of John and Ann Goode Andrews to reach middle age. John Andrews was a cotton planter of substantial means but with a rough and ready approach to society. Ann Andrews was described as more dignified and devout. The young Andrews grew to manhood on a plantation of some size and in a family of influence in the Wilkes County community composed of many transplanted Virginians like John Andrews. Garnett Andrews was educated at the Washington, Georgia, Academy, a well-respected institution certainly above the class of "old field schools" to which so many of his generation went.

He was married on 10 April 1828 to Annulet Ball, a lovely lady of "sherry colored eyes" and auburn hair, whose family was related to George Washington's mother. She was a student of history and of elegant manners and high breeding. Eliza Bowen, Garnett Andrews's niece who was reared with his children, described her as "one of the best wives that ever fell to the lot of any man, and when Judge Andrews's health or eyes incapacitated him, she read aloud to him, chiefly history, but also good novels. Among other accomplishments characteristic of a Southern woman whose husband was a large planter, she was an extremely skillful and patient nurse and also a pretty good physician." Bowen goes on to describe her as "not only handsome, with clear cut Grecian nose, but her good looks wore admirably."

There were eight children born of this union. Cora, the oldest child, was born in 1829. She later became the wife of Troup Butler and set up residence on the Butler Plantation near Albany, Georgia. The eldest son, John Frederick (born 1830), rose during the Civil War to the rank of lieutenant of artillery. A second son James Garnett lived only two years, dying in 1834, the same year that Henry Francis was born. Henry Francis Andrews studied at the University of Georgia and was graduated from the New York College of Physicians and Surgeons. He served two years as house physician at Bellevue Hospital in New York City and then returned to his home in Washington, Georgia. At the outbreak of war he volunteered as a private in the Irvin Guards, but soon was appointed surgeon with the military hospitals in Richmond. At the conclusions of hostilities he settled in his hometown to practice medicine and here he died in 1892. Garnett Andrews, Jr. (1837-1903) had just graduated from the University of Georgia School of Law when he joined the Georgia Light Artillery as lieutenant. In 1864 he was detailed at the rank of major to form the Second Foreign Legion, organized through the voluntary enlistment of foreigners among Federal prisoners of war. Popularly known as the "Galvanized Yankees" this unit fought a bloody battle against General Stoneman at Salisbury, North Carolina, on 11 April 1865, not knowing of General Lee's surrender two days earlier. Here Andrews was severely wounded. He soon moved to Yazoo City, Mississippi, where he established a successful law practice. He published *Andrews' Digest of the Decisions of the Supreme Court of Mississippi* in 1884. Married to the former Rosalie Champe Beirne, he moved in 1882 to Chattanooga, Tennessee, where again he developed a lucrative legal practice and served a term as mayor. A second daughter, Eliza Frances, "Fanny", was born 10 August 1840. She distinguished herself as a writer, teacher, and scholar, but is best known for her *War-Time Jounal of a Georgia Girl* (New York, 1908), one of the finest recollections of the Civil War. She also wrote three novels and two highly acclaimed textbooks of botany. In 1926 she was elected to the International Academy of Literature and Science in Italy. She died in Rome, Georgia, 21 January 1931. Metta, the youngest daughter, was born in 1845. It was she who, after marriage to Theodorick M. Green, came into possession of the family home, Haywood, and who long was a prominent citizen of Washington-Wilkes. The last child, Daniel Marshall, named for Garnett Andrews's physician brother, was too young to participate in the Civil War. He was particularly close to his sister Fanny. He later settled in Alabama.

Admitted to the bar in the early 1820's, Garnett Andrews first began his practice as an associate of Duncan Green Campbell, commissioner for the Creek Treaty of 1824 and

Georgia political leader. Campbell had been solicitor general of the Western Circuit from 1816 to 1819 and was state representative from Wilkes County from 1819-23 and 1825-26, serving as speaker pro-tem in 1825. Shortly after being nominated for governor Campbell died on 31 July 1828. Andrews, throughout his fifty years of law, formed several other partnerships, the longest being that with Isaiah Tucker Irvin, a Wilkes County state representative and speaker of the Georgia House of Representatives in 1859. Following Irvin's death, Andrews was, in 1860, elected to replace him as state representative.

From 1834 to 1845, 1853-1855, and again from 1868 until his death in 1873, he served as judge of the Northern Circuit of Georgia, which included Wilkes and the adjacent counties. The Northern Circuit had been formed in 1819, with Elbert, Hancock, Lincoln, Oglethorpe, Warren, and Wilkes, with Madison and Taliaferro added soon after by their formation. The first judge was John Mitchell Dooly who served until his death 26 May 1827, to be followed by William Harris Crawford who likewise served until his death on 15 September 1834. Andrews then succeeded to the office. Before taking his seat on the bench, he had practiced for a time in the north Georgia mountains, riding the circuit to Dahlonega often and becoming involved in litigations involving gold-mining rights in that area.

One of the more interesting of Judge Andrews's judicial decisions involved the question of disqualification of testimony given by one who was not a believer in future punishment and the Georgia law to that effect. About 1842 at a trial on the Northern Circuit, a witness was introduced who was a Universalist and the person against whom the testimony would have effect raised strong objection through his lawyer. The basis of objection was that since the witness was a well-known Universalist, his testimony according to Georgia law would be inadmissable because of the "belief in future punishment" clause. Judge Andrews, after consideration, ruled that the law of Georgia, as it then stood, disqualified this witness. Dr. L. F. W. Andrews (no relation to the Judge), a Universalist pamphleteer in Georgia, began a tirade against the ruling. In matter of fact, Judge Andrews was not in favor of the law but felt bound by his oath of office to uphold it despite his private notions of its propriety and justice. He stated that the best way to get a bad law repealed was to enforce it, and, in this case, it certainly occurred as the law was altered in the very next session of the legislature.

It has been said of Andrews that "no judge ever retained his ermine more unspotted, or left a more unsullied name behind him." A man of aristocratic bearing, he was rarely on the stronger side in politics, being defeated for governor in 1855 by Herschel V. Johnson. Andrews ran in that election on the American Party ticket, commonly called the Know-Nothings. Along with such associates as Benjamin Harvey Hill and Eugenius Aristides Nisbet, Andrews had joined the Know-Nothings during the Whig split following the Kansas-Nebraska bill of 1854. Andrews also supported strongly the new party's stand declaring the danger of unrestricted immigration. His friends Alexander Stephens and Robert Toombs, at the same time, chose to cast their lot with the Democrats. In the 1855 election, Andrews lost to Johnson by some 10,000 votes, while a third candidate, Basil Hallam Overby of the Temperance Party polled 6000 votes. In addition, Andrews was vehemently opposed to secession; he argued his case strongly while a member of the Georgia House in 1860, but resigned himself to the inevitability of secession.

Although disappointed, he did not object when his eldest sons almost immediately enlisted in the Confederate army or when his close friend Robert Toombs led the movement to secede. As his daughter, the novelist Eliza Frances Andrews, wrote about him, "He did his best to hold Georgia in the Union but he might as well have tried to tie up the

northwest wind in the corner of a pocket handkerchief."
Judge Andrews realized the inevitable failure of his desires.
On the evening of the celebration of Georgia's secession,
according to his daughter,

> he shut himself up in his house, darkened the windows, and paced up and down the room in the greatest agitation. Every now and then, when the noise of the shouting and the ringing of bells would penetrate to our ears through the closed doors and windows, he would pause and exclaim: Pool fools! They may ring bells now, but they will wring their hands - yes, and their hearts, too - before they are done with it.

Adding to the irony of Judge Andrews's convictions was the fact that the flag hoisted upon the naked shaft from which "Old Glory" had been pulled down, had been designed and sewn by the venerable judge's daughter and daughter-in-law. This "Bonnie Blue Flag" of a white star on a blue background waved proudly until replaced by the official Confederate "Stars and Bars."

The Andrews' home, Haywood, a stately plantation house with seven Doric columns across the front, became a haven for Southern families fleeing from the onslaught of war. Here along with the immediate Andrews family were various cousins and friends like Mary Day (later the wife of Sidney Lanier) of Macon and, at the close of the war, General Arnold Elzey of Maryland and his family.

Because of his Union sentiments and the fact that he maintained the respect of the local townspeople, Andrews was instrumental in eliminating much of the harshness of Reconstruction for Washington and Wilkes County. The judgeship he had resigned in 1855 to mount a gubernatorial campaign was once again his by 1868. He became a voice of sense and moderation in a critical period of the state's history.

He did, however, suffer extreme financial hardships in the years immediately following the war. Most of his funds had been invested in plantation lands and slaves, primarily in Mississippi. When the war ended, his property was in shambles and his investment in slaves completely lost. Even in such dire times, he still maintained his integrity and personal honesty absorbing large losses through the devaluation of Confederate currency. He was able, however, by sheer determination to bring to his family financial security with the reestablishment of his legal practice and his judgeship.

The author of articles for the *Southern Cultivator* and several speeches on agricultural subjects (a particular interest of this planter-lawyer), he is best remembered for the delightful *Reminiscences of an Old Georgia Lawyer* (Atlanta, 1870).

Andrews was a devoted father and husband. The death of his wife in the winter of 1872, was a tragedy from which he never recovered and he followed her to the grave on 14 August 1873.

As an unrecorded eulogizer has noted of Judge Andrews, The real business of his life was with the law and his greatest glory will ever be the incorruptible integrity with which he administered the high trust reposed in him for so many years - an integrity so pure and unassailable that not even the bitterest partisan spirit has ever tried to cast a stain upon it, and as long as his name is remembered in Georgia, it will be as a just and incorruptible judge - a man whose honor and purity were above all price.

            Robert M. Willingham, Jr.

PREFACE.

If there be but a step from the sublime to the ridiculous, there is but another between representing the latter and becoming its object, and I know I run the risk of finding myself in the latter predicament by recording what I have heard told with effect, but which may appear very flat, diluted with the ink of my pen.

I know there is no reputation to be made by retailing other men's wit, however successful, and much to be lost if unsuccessful. These admonitions would have kept me silent if I had had no object in view but placing this unpretending volume before the public; for the reader will do me great injustice to suppose I have the vanity to think these reminiscences, of themselves, merit a place before it. The true motive of publication will appear by reading the annexed advertisement.

Wishing to say nothing unpleasant to any one, I have to that end, in a few instances, had to use fictitious, instead of real names.

I hope the reader will bear in mind that it is impossible to write one's own reminiscences without a frequent and embarrassing use of the pronoun "I."

ADVERTISEMENT.

To the Lawyers of the United States:

The wit of the stage and literary men gives some of the most delightful reading in the English language, but, I think, inferior to that which might be had of our profession, if not lost—as much has been—to the world for want of record. I say lost to the world, because it is a gainer every time it is made to laugh, or is even amused. Besides, I think it due to the profession, that it should have credit for the many witty things it has said, as well as due to the world, that it should have the benefit of the many good ones we have seen and heard.

I have had the boldness—rather rashness—to commence the record on the scant material of a very uneventful, though long professional life, with the hope and expectation of aid from a generous and liberal profession. This beginning will indicate, partly, the character of the contributions I wish. I say partly, because I wish anything appertaining to the profession, whether comic, tragic, pathetic, curious or marvelous, which will interest the general reader.

Law reports give only so much of a case as may be necessary to present the law points involved, when some of them would be of great interest to the general reader if reported with that view alone. I know of nothing which would make a better history of the state of society in a country than selections from its law suits. For what is "found in the by-ways rather than in the main-roads of history" is often most interesting to a majority of readers. Without pretending to write history, I wish everything pertaining to the profession, of the above character, that I may select what I think worth presenting to the public.

There is, with the profession, a rich store of material for the amusement and instruction of the world, if it will yield it up. Not expecting, nor wishing to tax the time and attention of gentlemen, so constantly engaged as the profession generally is, I desire to pay liberally for all contributions received, which I may use; and I would be pleased to have contributors price their own labors, and consent that I may give their address.

Address   GARNETT ANDREWS,
Washington, Ga.

CONTENTS.

CHAPTER I.

Introduction.—An old friend's yarn about old times—Peach Brandy Baptists—African slave trade—The war of 1812, and the mails—Corn-shuckings—The Baptist meetings—The first riding vehicle ever seen at a country church—Double log cabbins, sandy floors, pewter ware and tinkers—Advantages of a new country—Curse of a new county—"Bob" Martin's account of 100 lbs. of brown sugar and pair of silver-plated stirrup-irons.

CHAPTER II.

A glance at Law, Lawyers' habits, &c., during half a century past.—Decline in respect for the law and its officers—Old rules of court—Separate table for the bar—Punishment for contempts—Sheriffs waited on the Judges—Sheriff of new county—Parade and ceremony; Judiciary entitled to respect; Independence of Judges—Violence—Bribery of Judges—How laws evaded—State of law when I came to the bar—Improvement since—Religion and habits of old lawyers—Mode of travel—The wreck—Lawyers last circuit—Gamblers—Green-bags—Fiddler Billy—Popular oratory—Taverns.

CHAPTER III.

Justices' Courts.—The young lawyers toughest case—A court broke up in a row—Deliberation and impetuosity—Miss Nancy Rumsey and the Irishman—Strange names of districts—Wolf Skin—The Lick—Dooley District.

CHAPTER IV.

The Northern Circuit.—Leading members of the Northern bar half a century since—First records of Wilkes county—Judge Dooley, his birth, education, habits and talents—Tom Peter Carnes

—He and Dooley practice in South Carolina—Carnes' speech on a syllogism—Charles and the lawyers at breakfast—Singular treatment of slaves—Dooley's speech on the nuncupative will—A will made at the bottom of a well—Dooley's happy manner of saying things—Corn good enough for his horse—Joltees—Don't let him shoot this way—Comparison between Dooley and Charles the Second—Mr. Sheriff, some more water out of that same well—How Dooley tried to stop gambling—His fight with Long. Tait challenges him. Moves to a tavern where he will be considered a gentleman—Dooley's interviews with the roast pig—Rivalry between the village taverns and discomfiture of the little widow—Dooley gets the laugh on a young lawyer. Dooley and the brass-heeled Doctor—How he punishes his neighbor, hunting Mark Bond—Judge Crawford succeeds Dooley. How rapidly he rose in life—His appearance, his character, his greatness and talents—He and the lawyer who repeated his arguments. His treatment of Clark men—Reply to his priest-ridden landlady—Fatal meeting with Van Allen—Characteristic interview with Mr. Dawson—He, Van Allen and Gov. Clark—He brings the first *ne exeat* in Georgia—The defendant and Martin at the corn-shucking—General Heard and his suit—Phil. Alston and his amusing originality—How Heard tried to marry off a Militia Captain, and drunken dependent, and how he prospered—Speech of old Peter Bnnett, the Constable.

CHAPTER V.

The Middle Circuit.—Leading lawyers—Ned Bacon—The staunch old Methodist and rebel preacher—The young convict.

CHAPTER VI.

The Western Circuit.—Early discovery of gold—Cheerful feelings in the mountains—Sensations excited by viewing mountain scenery—Advantages of Middle Georgia, from the falls of her great rivers to the mountains—The place for the U. S. Capitol. Most pleasant recollections of my professional life—Population of the newly discovered mines—Court scenes—Cynthia Hyde and Polly Heflin—A Spooney wishes to play cards, and how he succeeds—Lewie, the fiddler, at the camp dances—He and a North Carolina "laddie" test their literary attainments—His misfortunes—Letter to Lewic—Col. Stamper—How he won a wife, and how he was transformed from a singing-master into a lawyer and Militia Colonel—His speeches and exploits—Judge Underwood—Visit to Rabun as a lawyer—Tiger-tail and War-woman's creeks—Judge "T." rides the Western Circuit, his originality—Sulphur and a clean shirt—Amusing charges by Judges—Visit to Rabun as Judge—Serenaded—Trick of a waggish lawyer—A circumstantial account of the great battle between a Methodist Circuit Rider and the Blacksmith of Rabun Gap—What the Gap was and what it will be—The preacher and Jack Hawks—Reasons why lawyers' social intercourse is easy and agreeable—Top duck at last—Trouble of having a reputation to sustain—The dog Rackett—Widows' taverns—Judge Clayton, his character and anecdotes—The applicant for admission to the church—The negro's sermon—The man who was reading Riley's narrative—Organization of Rabun county and the boy with the cotton rag.

CHAPTER VII.

Lawyers' fees—Lawyers' profits.

REMINISCENCES OF AN OLD GEORGIA LAWYER.

CHAPTER I.

Introduction.—An old friend's yarn about "old times"—Peach brandy Baptists—African slave trade—The war of 1812 and the mails—Corn-shuckings—The Baptist meetings—The first riding vehicle ever seen at a country church. Double log cabins, sandy floors, pewter-ware and tinkers—Advantages of a new country—Curse of a new county—"Bob" Martin's account of 100 lbs. of brown sugar, and a pair of silver-plated stirrup-irons.

Much of that about which I write, occurred some years before my professional life began, and was told me by others, and as some idea of the general state of society at that time is a very proper introduction to my professional reminiscences, I give that from a like source.

An old friend—like many old people—was bewailing the degeneracy of the times; but more particularly the consequences of making a new county—Talliaferro—in the limits of which he had been caught. Some how or other he connected, not only his own, but the misfortunes of the country, with the county-lines which had been drawn around him.

The extreme limits of five counties made the new one; and the people in them, living remotely from towns, were free from the vices and extravagances of such corrupting neighborhoods, and were of great simplicity and purity of manners, as will appear in a conversation I had with "the old friend," by the fire-side, one winter night. I will give—after many years—what I now remember of his yarn:

"My parents were from "Old Virginia," and of the Baptist persuasion. My father was—what was called—"an old peach brandy Baptist;" by which I mean, he made peach brandy, kept it on his side-board, took a drink before breakfast and dinner, and asked every one who came to his house to do the same, particularly the preachers, who drank, and as they drank, became more happy and fervently religious. In my simplicity I did not then know what was the matter, but I have long since learned better. I don't care if the spirit which increased their religious demonstrations, did come out of my father's decanter, they were, nevertheless, good men and Christians.

My first recollections go back to about the time of closing the African slave trade, in 1808, when the country was full of "outlandish" or "new negroes," as they were called. I remember how many professed to have been Princes and Princesses in their own country; how they had marks of distinction on their flesh—as they said; how many of them were rotten with cutaneous diseases; how many destroyed their lives to return to their own country; how some large slaveholder arrested it by cutting off the head of a suicide and telling the survivors he would return to his country without it, and that he would decapitate all self-destroyers in the same way; how some trader had given his purchased slaves pants to hide their nakedness, and on the next morning found them tied around their necks as ornaments; how one ran away, got frost-bitten, cut off his feet and placed them before the fire, and many other like marvellous stories.

I remember the war of 1812, with its privations and hardships; how I was going to school, and cyphering in long division, and learning grammar—and thought to be a prodigy of learning—at a house on the great public road, leading from Augusta, by Washington, to Greensboro; how the mail came to Washington once a week, staid all night and went thirty miles next day to Greensboro, with all the letters and papers for all the country, in a pair of common saddle-bags; how the war news was a month coming from the "Niagara frontier;" how my father took two newspapers, the only ones to be had for many miles around; how the neighbors came to hear the news, and how we school-boys, all admired the brave mail-boy, who had to travel that thirty miles, rain or shine, and even in the night, if any accident happened, and hence, he could halloo the challenge of "school-butter" with impunity, as we stood in too much awe of such bravery and the United States, to molest him.

The only festivities or entertainments of the country, besides an occasional wedding, were corn-shuckings and Baptist "meetings"—as then called—for the "Baptists and crab-grass" had taken all the land then cleared in the country.

I have often sat on my father's stile, during the nights of November and December, and listened to the corn-songs floating on the frosty night-air from some neighbor's corn-pile—for the voice of the negroes were generally musical, and strong as a steam whistle.

When starting for the festivity—for the shuckings were so considered—a solitary refrain might be heard a mile or two away, then another would join, and as they approached, more and more, until they arrived, singing, at the corn-pile in a company of fifteen or twenty; sometimes two or three of such companies would approach at the same time, making the night-air resonant with melody—I say melody, for I know of no music so melodious to my ear, at a short distance, as an old time corn-song. Arriving at the corn-pile, some leader—by common tacit consent—assumed the office of "General," which was to "give out." "Giving out" was a recitative which he remembered, or made—according to the inspiration of the moment—when the great ring around the corn-pile answered in the chorus of "Ha, Hi, Ho." I remember one ran thus :

"Did you ever hear the cow laugh?
"Ha, Hi, Ho,
"And how you think the cow laugh?
"Ha, Hi, Ho,
"The cow say moo, moo, moo,
"Ha, Hi, Ho,
"And what you think the cow want?
"Ha, Hi, Ho,
"The cow want corn and that what the cow want;
"Ha, Hi, Ho.

The "General" would continue to express the same solicitude for such of the corn-eating animals, as he might sympathise with, until satisfied.

Most of the planters having come from Virginia and made money, first by growing tobacco and then cotton, would go back to that State and Maryland and buy slaves; Hence, many of their songs referred to old "Virginny," Richmond and Baltimore.

The "General," sticking a corn-shuck in his hat, by way of distinction, would mount the corn-pile and frequently, in his recitative, address the ring as his children, his soldiers or his army. Sometimes he would, in the enthusiasm of the occasion, fall on his knees and clap his hands above his head, then rise, holding them, clasping a ear of corn, in the same attitude, then with legs in the form of the letter V inverted, and his left arm akimbo—all the time "giving out"—he would wave his right, in his rhapsody, gracefully—as if monarch of all he surveyed; then, with a stage-strut, he would move to another part of the pile to encourage his soldiers there, and picking up another ear and holding it with out-stretched arm, high above his head, would lean back, as if gazing at the stars behind him, and go through such other extravagant attitudes as the genius of the actor and fervor of the moment might inspire.

During the shucking the planter, his son or overseer would visit, occasionally, the ring, with the bottle, when the shucking would become "fast and furious," and if not taken round often enough, the "General" would put a petition or remonstrance on the subject into his recitative.

At the end of the shucking, came the chairing of the planter, his son, or overseer, around the "big.house," accompanied by an appropriate corn-song. And finally came the supper in the kitchen, when the enjoyment was at the highest.

Since "freedom came about," the old corn-song seems to have died out with slavery. Its sound now would seem like a voice from the grave of the buried feudal power and wealth of the old slave holders.

In the country where I was raised, remote from towns and villages, the big Baptist "meetings" were the only other convivial gatherings—I say convivial, not that there was not as much deep religious exercises as I ever saw, but because it was for these occasions the turkeys, eggs and fatted calves were kept, to entertain friends coming from a distance. It was going to and returning from these "meetings," on horseback, that all the courting of the young people was done. One of the most dexterous and admired feats of gallantry was, for a young spark to cut out his rival—that is to ride between him and his girl as their horses watered at a creek, or on some other sought for occasion.

My mother was a pious and very religious Baptist woman—they had not then fallen from the dignity of womanhood to ladyhood*—whose main enjoyment in life was attending Baptist "meetings."

My father, an enterprising well-to-do man, had made for her what was then called a chair, (pronounced cheer,) and afterwards a gig. It was constructed of ash, by a common wagon-maker of the country, without springs, and painted blue, like the wagons and split-bottom chairs so common throughout the Southern country; the body was what, I think, is called a stool body, after the fashion of the old sulkies. My father had, almost, everything manufactured on his plantation; among the rest, his own flax, leather and shoes. Dick, his shoemaker, made the harness for the chair. Some of the negroes of the plantion, made the "wahoo"

---

*If the Bible was now translated into modern English, as spoken on this side the Atlantic, it would read in this way: "The rib, which the Lord God had taken from the gentleman, made He a lady and brought her unto the gentleman. . . . And the gentleman said, the lady Thou gavest me . . . And the Lord God said unto the lady, what is this thou hast done? and the lady said, the serpent beguiled me . . . . . King Solomon loved many strange ladies, &c." Then Herod, when he had called the wise gentlemen, enquired, &c.

I have heard of lawyers, referring to a vagabond thief on trial, calling him "the gentleman on trial."

A freedman came to my neighbor, Mrs. B., and said he wanted "to see the woman who, he understood, wished to hire a lady to cook for her." I thought he was of unusual taste and discrimination, and was pleased with the compliment he paid Mrs. B., in classing her among the women.

collar. The reins, I do not recollect, but have no doubt they were a pair of cotton plow lines.

Whatever moderns may think of the turn-out, thus far, we had a splendid, docile grey horse, that could rival the best of his successors now. The grey was hitched in this spanking new equipage and I—then in robin-hood—was selected to drive mother to her old "meeting house" (Watley's, now Bethesda,) in this, the first wheeled vehicle—made as a luxury for riders—that had ever approached its sacred precincts.

Tom Hunt, a boy a few years older than I, had aroused the envy, not to say hatred, of all the boys for wearing to school a pair of coarse boots, made by Jack, his father's shoemaker. The pleasure of the ride, with whip in hand, had been delicious, but as I passed Tom with his boots, I had a feeling of triumph that was new and delightful. This was but the beginning of the triumphs, of that, the great day of my life. I took pains to drive up as near the front door of the "meeting house"—as it was then called—as propriety would permit, to the end that my turn-out might be seen by everybody in general, and Jinny Shotwell in particular, who, I thought, had looked with tender emotions on Tom's boots the Sunday before.

The morning sermon was, as usual, long—to me—an age in length. When it was ended the congregation dispersed to get water, eat lunch, but above all, to see the great show in the yard. Soon there was a large crowd gathered round the chair, that would not now be considered good enough for an apple cart. Old Elijah Dearing, a very tall man, with a very long walking stick, was the leading surveyor in examining the strange contrivance. Just before, I had noticed that Jinny had passed by and lingered, too, to admire. Tom was standing by, and looked as enviously at the chair as ever I had at the boots. After Mr. D. had looked at, and shaken the thing, he straightened his long limber body up, tapped a spoke of the wheel with his long stick, and exclaimed, "Well! well!! what will this world come to next." Then my feelings were worth five dollars per minute, and though I am near my three score and ten, I have not been as happy since. Why should I not have been the happiest of boys, or men either? There was the love of Jinny Shotwell, the mortification of my rival, Tom Hunt, and the admiration of all the world besides, secured in one moment, with the tallest man in the country endorsing the completeness of my turn-out. It has fallen to the lot of no boy, or man, whom I have known, to have been the subject of so many great triumphs at the same time. I have said when I drove through my father's gate, that morning, with my spanking equipage I was in robin-hood, when I returned, I was in all the pride and insolence of puppy-hood. So much had one eventful day advanced me towards manhood.

During the war of 1812, all the goods we received in the interior of Georgia, came out in the peddlers' wagons from the New England States, and in a few wagons that carried cotton to Baltimore, (600 miles,) and returned laden with merchandise.

There was a merchant in the neighborhood named Shorter, who had a daughter Kate, who, through the peddlers' or her father's wagons, had become the owner of a parasol, the first that had ever been seen in all that vicinity, and the possession of which had made her as odious, among the girls, as Tom Hunt's boots had made him among the school-boys. Though every damsel in the neighborhood was plaiting oat-straw bonnets and spinning jeans cloth to buy a parasol, they had been diligently engaged in ridiculing poor Kate's "rag," which it seems she stretched and flourished on every possible occasion. She was in danger of having an edict of excommunication issued against her, by the feminines visiting that church, until my dear old mother came to her relief. For she soon made a diversion in Miss Kate's favor. The envy and ridicule of the sisterhood were now turned against the owner of the chair. The doctrine of election and final perseverance, forbade that she should have "fallen from grace," but she had become "too proud and worldly minded for a Christian," and they were "greatly hurt." *They* could go to an Association, for three to four days, with clothes in a pocket handkerchief suspended to the horns of their saddles, "but sister S. must have a trunk tied on to her two-wheeled wagon for hers." "Pride would have a fall," for they greatly feared the " chair" would turn over, or the horse run away and break "the dear sister's neck;" for which some, I fear, would have been thankful to God, as a just judgment on a haughty spirit.

As my good and inoffensive mother had made a diversion in favor of poor Kate, so the leading Baptist preacher came to her relief.

He was deputed by the church to attend a Convention, or some other Ecclesiastical body, at Philadelphia, when he, too, had a chair for him and his wife to take the journey in. He left in a shad-breasted jeans coat—which all the preachers then wore, and, in warm weather, laid off in the pulpit—and his wife, with a plain ribbon to her bonnet; but, to the great scandal of religion, he returned with lapells to his broadcloth coat, and she, not only with colored ribbons, but sinful bows on a new bonnet. In this greater sin, of the greater luminaries of the church, my dear mother was almost forgotten, and suffered to travel to all the "big meetings" in comparative peace.

If these old preachers did fight the devil with coats off, it was to some purpose, for I have never known a more religious and moral community, nor one more deeply impressed with the truths of the Bible and religion, than the people under their ministrations.

Those were the days of double log cabins and sanded floors; of burnished pewter plates, displayed to the sun and passers-by, on a shelf at the front door, and to visitors in an open cupboard in the principal room of the house; and of tinkers, with their packs on their backs, to mend such wares as might be broken, or to mold new ones for the thrifty house-wives.

I have not seen a pewter plate, nor a tinker, within these new county lines since they were run.

Those were the days when the land was fresh from the hand of God—no Sedge nor Bermuda grass—and the country covered with cane and magnificent forests, and the rivers and creeks full of shad and other fish.

If a young man wished to marry he went on the other side of the spring—or to another on his father's abundant, cheap, rich, virgin soil—built his log cabin, cleared a turnip-patch and cowpen, married and went to multiplying and replenishing the earth.

Since these new county lines, the country is scarred with red gullies, the cane, forests and fish gone, and if a young man marries he may expect to feed his children on red clay and blackberries.

They got their new county, and not only reaped all these bitter fruits—and more of others than I can mention—but have lost their simple and industrious habits. The boys must quit the plow and go to town, and learn to drink, dance and play cards. Because they have a court-house, neighbors, who used to settle their little disputes in the church, have gone to law. One-half bought dry goods and liquor—and bad liquor at that—and the other half went to buying and drinking, and they all broke; brethren who had belonged to the same church and lived neighbors all their lives without an unkind word, went to lying and fighting over the new county offices. And here we are—once the happiest and most independent people in the world, now the most miserable set of poor devils on the earth, and all on account of these new county lines they have run around us."

Here my old friend groaned aloud, re-filled his pipe, and in his agony of soul puffed smoke like a steam-engine.

In corroboration of my old friend's account of the simplicity of his neighbors, of half a century since, "Bob Martin," late Clerk of the Supreme Court of the State, who lived in Greene county, and not more than ten or twelve miles from my old friend, said that the Methodists turned the principal citizen of the county out of their church for buying a hundred pounds of brown sugar at one time.

He told, in his inimitable way, how the congregation of a country church was broken up by a pair of silver-plated stirrup irons, in the following way :

A country beau had given out, that when he sold his cotton, he would buy a pair of silver-plated stirrup irons. This was "no-rated about," and disputed by some, who said, extravagant as he might be and as fine as his horse was, he would not be such a spendthrift as to throw away money so foolishly as that. Others taking the affirmative side with equal warmth, it occasioned a stirrup and anti-stirrup party in the neighborhood, that would have created great strife, had not events soon put the question to rest.

It was known that the prodigal had gone to Augusta to sell his cotton, and on his return would be at a certain country church at the coming "meeting." He went, he sold, he returned. When next Sunday came, there was the largest congregation in attendance that was ever known at that church within the memory of the oldest inhabitant. The preacher did not commence his services until some half hour after the usual time, the expected beau not having arrived, and knowing the expectations of the large congregation in attendance. The important gentleman, wishing to create as great a sensation as the splendor of his equipments would justify, delayed his arrival until every one should be on the ground. After the preacher commenced his services, the silver-plated stirrups, with the beau came, who, tying his horse in a conspicuous place, first one saw and went to examine the wonder, and then another, and another, until the preacher was left without a congregation.

CHAPTER II.

A glance at law, lawyers and their habits during half a century past—Decline in respect for the law and its officers—Old rule of Court—Separate table for the Bar—Punishment for contempts—Sheriffs waited on Judges—Sheriff of new county—Parade and ceremony—Judiciary entitled to respect—Independence of the Judges—Violence—Bribery of Judges—How laws are evaded—State of the law when I came to the Bar—Improvement since.—Religion and habits of old Lawyers—Mode of travel—The wreck—Lawyers' last Circuit—Gamblers—Green-bags—Fiddler Billy—Popular oratory—Taverns.

A foreigner, giving an account of his travels in the United States, and remarking on the decline of respect shown for authority, said, when we came out of the revolution the citizens had been subjects, and the people, substituting George Washington and the officers of the government for George the Third and the colonial officials, gave the former the same respect they had the latter. Time, with the operation of democratic institutions, has worn away all the awe, not to say respect, once shown high official station, so that a Judge of the Superior Court and his Sheriff have now, hardly more respect shown them than was formerly considered the due of a Justice of the Peace and his Constable.

On the 26th of January, 1790, at Wilkes Superior Court, the following order was passed, and has never been revoked: "For a direct conformity to ancient custom, and for a necessary distinction in the profession, the attorneys shall be heard in the causes of their clients, in the habit of a black robe; but this not to be insisted on with those who shall not have provided themselves with such habits, until the second term. A further rule shall provide for the mode of recognizing Barristers and establishing other necessary distinctions."

The enforcement of the above rule now, would be followed, if not by a riot, by a general burst of ridicule that would prompt the "gentlemen of the black gown" soon to apply for its revocation.

Formerly it was very common to give the Judge and Bar separate tables at the hotels, and in allusion to this distinction, Judge Cone used to say, "instead of separate tables, this was the last generation of lawyers that would be permitted to sit at the first."

Much of this is because the Judges have been almost entirely shorn of their common law power of punishing for contempts. The Sheriffs, who, long since my recollection, by themselves or Deputy, and sometimes both, always escorted the Judges to and from their quarters—and I knew one who made them convey him from one court house to the next, until the riding was completed —have now generally dispensed with what they consider as a useless ceremony.

I knew one Sheriff—the first of a new county—highly appreciating his new dignity, when the Judge first came to organize it, met him armed with his sword and decorated "*cap-a-pie*," including the cocked-hat, with the gaudy uniform (but for its rust) of a Captain of Cavalry. But he never faced the jeers of "the boys" but that one time.

Those who look on all the imposing forms and ceremonies—not to say pomp—with which official station in some countries is, and once in this was, clothed, as empty parade, take a very superficial view of human nature; for the more awe with which authority is invested, the less necessity will there be for its actual exercise; moral power will peaceably effect what physical force otherwise would—often with violence—have to accomplish.

Of all departments of our Government—State and National—the Judiciary is the most important, and I think it has wonderfully vindicated its claim to popular respect and confidence, and all admit that it is of the first importance that its independence should be secured. But the popular idea of independence is that it should have an adequate salary, not only that the Judges may appropriate the whole of their time to the discharge of official duty, but be free from great temptations of bribery; and that the tenure of office should be such that they should be under no temptation to use corrupt means to obtain a new investiture of their station. There are other motives that will impair his independence as much as an insufficient salary or insecure tenure of office.

Many men will shrink from personal insult and violence as much as from want or a deprivation of office; and it is better to arm the Judge with an almost arbitrary power of punishment than risk the want of such protection. A Judge, to be independent, should be under no necessity of vindicating his official conduct by his pen, tongue or arm, except before the high Court of Impeachment, the responsibility to which is sufficient security against his abuse of power. The people have ten times more interest in his absolute independence—save as above excepted—than in any apprehended abuse of power. A Judge should not only be free from insult and violence, but from the fear of them, and NOT for *his* sake but for that of the suitors in his court.

I knew a Judge who had his face spit upon, in going from his quarters to the court-house. If the Sheriff had been in the place, which ancient form, (as the unthinking would call it) or the office invested with its ancient dignity, awe and power, the indignity would not have occurred. It was but the other day, as reported by the newspapers, a Judge—for fining a young man for contempt, was attacked by him, and standing in defiance of the Sheriff, he was unable to arrest the offender.

During a seat on the bench of the Superior Court, of some fifteen or twenty years, I was threatened with violence twice. Once by a convict whom I had sentenced to the penitentiary, and who died before his term of imprisonment expired; and once by a desperado whom I had sent to jail for contempt, and whom, while drunk, (and crossing it,) a friendly creek kindly took off my hands, before he carried his threat into execution.

I have never heard of but one Judge, in the State, who had been offered a bribe, and of but one suspected—and I think improperly —of having received it. But on several occasions court-houses have been burned, bidders deterred from bidding at Sheriff sales, and Sheriffs and Clerks have resigned to embarrass the collection of debts.

I regret to say, that within my experience, I have noticed a decline, not only in the respect due, and once paid Courts of Justice, but, as a necessary consequence, the law itself; and, I apprehend, this will be found true of all the old Colonial States.

When I came to the bar, and for years after, we had no digest of the laws, nor Supreme Court—every Circuit Judge being supreme in the counties over which he presided—and not even rules of practice. For want of the first, the lawyers had to go through all the statutes to make up an opinion on statute law; for want of the second, there were no precedents of adjudicated cases, by State courts, to be relied on as guides, and for want of the last, a lawyer was in the dark, often, how to conduct his pleadings or prepare his interrogatories. The consequence of this was, that hardly half the litigated cases were tried on their merits. For a lawyer, who had travelled the circuit and noted some unrecorded opinions given by the Judge as to the admission of interrogatories, evidence or amendment of pleadings, as well as upon great common or statute law questions, would frequently throw out of Court the most important cases without touching their merits. Now, with our Digests, Code, Reports of cases decided by the Supreme Court, and rules of Court, a case hardly ever is tried but on a full investigation of its true issues.

The main objection to the Supreme Court was that it would increase litigation and expense, but, on the contrary, I am confident it has greatly diminished both. Besides all this, there is a liberality of the profession in conducting business, almost unknown to the sharp practice of the old lawyers, who, fighting under the black flag, neither gave nor asked quarter. So, taking all these things together, with the general simplification of the mode of procedure adopted by our legislation, I think there is no country in which the common law is administered more speedily, cheaply and fairly than in Georgia.

With the increase of statutes, of decided cases, at home and abroad, and the multiplication of law books in general, have come better lawyers; for so many points and principles have been settled and recorded that the industrious lawyer will generally find something, partly or wholly, to control his case, which formerly would have depended on an argument on general principles by counsel. And though, for the above reasons, this generation of lawyers may be superior to their predecessors as lawyers, they are not as advocates, if their equals.

Nearly half a century since, when I came to the Georgia Bar, I recollect but two lawyers of my circuit who were members of the church. Now, I think, the profession is as well represented there—except by the ministry, of course—as any in the State.

Spirits were always placed in our rooms, as well as in the bars of the hotels at which we stopped, and whist was a common amusement at night, though not much betting, but now cards and spirits have long since been almost entirely banished from the lawyers' rooms.

In my first recollection most of the lawyers travelled the circuit on horseback, then sulkies became general, and then buggies and railroads succeeded them. During the sulky reign, some seven or eight were going to Lincoln court, when Judge Lumpkin—our late Chief Justice—upset his, and there being six more before him, his horse running away drove them all (in point of time) to follow his example, when we had seven wrecked sulkies and as many frightened horses and lawyers. From this time we dated, from the wrecked-riding, as the old people in Georgia did from the Yazoo fresh, and the big May frost, and as we do, and will for a long time, from "the surrender."

Speaking of sulkies reminds me of an instance of Judicial humor worth recording. An old lawyer, concluding on a younger member who had advanced some very extravagant doctrines, said he had seen a very fine painting called "The Lawyers' last Circuit," which consisted of a representation, in the background, of the flames of hell, into which a long row of lawyers in sulkies, seemed to be driving furiously, with a little devil holding each, and in the front the Judge, with two holding him securely, and he thought if his young friend had been represented in the group he would have been entitled to the distinction of three devils.

His Honor, the Judge, said he wished it understood that the Judges of this day were not so unmanageable as then, and that his Satanic Majesty should know they were not entitled to such distinguished consideration as their predecessors.

The gamblers or "sporting gentlemen"—as they were called—went the circuits almost as regularly as the lawyers, driving spanking equipages and always with finer clothes, and generally with more money than the gentlemen of the "green-bag."

Speaking of green-bags, reminds me to say, that, until a late day, every lawyer carried his papers in a wallet, generally of that color, and they were known as "gentlemen of the green-bag."

These "sporting gentlemen" were generally fine looking men, often of fine address and talents. Sometimes they gave such of the lawyers, as afforded them the chance, demonstrable evidence that they were as sharp in their profession as the gentlemen of the bar in theirs. I was told of one Solicitor General who, generally "out of stakes," would trade *nolle prosequis* to the gamblers for them—for there were generally a crop of indictments against the latter—so the price of *nolle prosequis*, depending on the State of the Solictor's purse, had a quotable, and quite as fluctuating a price among gamblers, during the circuit, as cotton, stocks or government bonds.

Fifty years since, there was an interloper who rode the Northern Circuit as regularly as the lawyers, and was quite as important as any who travelled it. The courts being generally enlivened by balls and dancing parties, "the fiddler" was in great demand. Now, it so chanced that four miles below Washington, Wilkes county, at a place known as "Log Hall," (where—said Mr. Prince—"the black-jacks were so crooked they would not lie still when cut down,") there lived a great musician in the person of an ugly negro called "Billy, the fiddler," or "Fiddler Billy," who, as well by playing for the dancers as for the idlers about the court yard, and amusing them with his wit—for he had the reputation of being a great wit—was able to travel the circuit in as good style as the lawyers. Billy's master, having been a convivial old Virginia horse-racer, encouraged him in his musical propensities. Billy was often very noisy in the court yard, and on one occasion so much so, that the Judge ordered the Sheriff to give him thirty-nine lashes. It happening at a time when "the alleviating law" protected debtors from paying but one-third of their debts annually—and which was called "the thirding law"—Billy stopped the Sheriff at the thirteenth stroke, and claimed the benefit of its merciful provisions, and on appealing to the Judge, he decided that Billy should have the advantages of its alleviating terms.

On another occasion he had a large company of boys, and other idlers, following him in the streets of Elberton, as he played "the fox and hounds," when a very conscientious Justice of the Peace, thinking the disorder should be abated, considered it his duty to have the musician arrested, and not finding the crime laid down in "the Georgia Justice," made out a warrant against him for "*Interlusine conduct.*"

There used to be current a great many anecdotes of "Billy the fiddler" and his wit, but the above will suffice to indicate what manner of negro he was.

The lawyers of that day differed from those of the present in not practicing popular oratory "from the stump." I do not remember to have heard, or to have heard of, any one canvassing from that forum prior to the advent of nullification. With that doctrine came popular oratory as a means of winning the "sweet voices" of the people. Though I recollect the barbecue, the grocery-treats and such like convivial political entertainments, at which candidates "most did congregate," and in which they participated, I have no recollection of "the gift of the gab" being called into requisition. It was not thought a necessary accomplishment for our early Presidents and Governors, nor important, even, for members of Congress, to be "gifted" in that way. Our people did not then, as now, graduate a man's talents by his tongue only. Men of worth, learning and station had a fair chance for office, though not winning of speech. Now, if Washington were living, with all his prestige, I don't know but he might be turned down, by the popular vote of a county, where all the voters could be addressed by a second-rate lawyer who might "get the grin against him from the stump."

Until Howell Cobb's candidacy, in eighteen hundred and fifty-one, no candidate for Governor, in Georgia, had—unless it may have been Townes—canvassed from the stump; and, I believe, Mr. Douglass was the first Presidential candidate who sought votes from the same stage. The consequence now is, the popular orators, on account of their valuable party services, have a monopoly of all the high offices, and they being, almost always lawyers, the United States Government has come under the control wholly, and the State Government partly, of the gentlemen of "the bar."

If government has to fall into the hands of any one profession it would be well it should be that of the lawyers, on account of the character of their studies, their liberality, intelligence and—which may appear incredible to some—their honesty. But on account of the incompatibility between the elements which make a popular orator and sound judgment, it is very perilous to have a government in the control of such unsafe hands. For the fervor which "comes from the heart and goes to the heart," unhinges the judgment, and the intensity of feeling and conviction which sends the words "two feet into the ground" at every sentence, sends everything with them "into the ground." It has become as common as a proverb to compliment a man's talents, accompanied by a regret that "he wants common sense," which being interpreted, means, he wants judgment. A popular orator hardly ever dies wealthy, though millions may have passed through his hands, out of which he might have honestly saved a fortune, and all for the want of judgment; for they all want and need money more than most men. Some one has said a statesman cannot afford to have passions—an orator cannot afford to be without them.

It has been charged by foreigners that the United States has not contributed its share to the arts, learning and science, though making better practical use of the last than any other people; for which various excuses have been rendered. If it be true, the reason is, that here, prolitics being open to all and so captivating to the ambitious, that nearly all the talent of the country is turned in that direction, to the great neglect of those things, which in monarchies—particularly absolute monarchies—are the only fields for the exercise of intellectutal ambition. A cart load of manure, under all circumstances, is of positive benefit to a country, the most eloquent speech ever made may be—as many have been—a curse.

Jimmy Potter having been asked to vote for Mr. Grattan, he wished to know what Mr. Grattan had ever done for him, and when told he was a great orator, and an honor to Ireland, Jimmy replied: "orathery—orathery; now look here sir, if there's anything I detest in this world, it is that same orathery. And if the King on his throne, or the Judge on his bench, was to say, what's the ruin of Ireland? by virtue of my oath, I'd say, its orathery; divil a thing else but orathery!"

"If Ireland is in danger of ruin by 'orathery,' what is to become of this gab-afflicted country?"

I met with the above anecdote in an English magazine, which gave another of "Orathery" in America.

Some one rose, in the midst of a crowd at an execution and said, "Brother Crane, having yet four minutes before he is turned off, will favor us with a few remarks on the new tariff."

I shall expect next the passengers on board a vessel about foundering in mid ocean, to call a meeting on deck, when a popular orator will mount a box, with a string of resolutions, with "appropriate whereases," and go down with a half finished sentence, in favor of his favorite candidate for President, on his lips.

My complaint is not so much of oratory in itself, when fairly conducted—for there is no other way to instruct the great mass of voters—but it is to making blatancy a standard for a fitness for all high employments; for many of the most talented, trustworthy and business men of the country, make no pretensions to the divine and enviable gift. Though a man cannot be an orator without talents, it does not follow that he may not be talented without oratory. In representative governments, like England and the United States, if there be any statesmen they are almost necessarily orators, because hardly any others can attain to high employments. In monarchies it is different; neither Richelieu, Tallyrand nor Bismark are known as orators. Can't that inconsiderate philanthropist who teaches the dumb to speak, be stopped, and directed to making the speakers dumb?

The first rudiments of tavern keeping used to be, and is now, occasionally, in some parts of Georgia, to begin with clean tablecloths once a week, "coffee tasting too strong of water," a tin wash basin in the piazza, with an endless towel on a roller, to be replaced with a clean one every Sunday morning; sheets changed when very much soiled, and without reference to the previous number of occupants; curtainless windows, dingy with fly-specks, and offensively unwashed waiters.

Where the city of Atlanta now stands I once knew a servant to come into a lady's bed-room and begin to smell the sheets, and on being asked, "why such scenting?" she answered, that a "sick man had been lying on the bed, and Missus had sent her to discover if the sheets smelled of Sperits of Turpentine, that they might be changed if they did."

Judge Cone once ordered a foot bath at a village tavern, and the water was brought by one, who seemed to be a corn-field negro, clad in a long-tailed, snuff colored jeans coat, shed by the landlord, for the benefit of Jim on court occasions. When he had washed the Judge's feet, and was told to wipe them, he brought round the tail of the jeans coat for the purpose; the Judge—who had a keen sense of the ludicrous,—jerked away his foot, and breaking into a laugh, apprised Jim that the long-tailed, snuff colored was not the proper thing; the latter answering with a prompt apology—to indicate that he knew what was right—said, "I have no handkercher, Mass Judge, or I would have used it." The Judge, bursting into another convulsion, was able in the intervals of his paroxism to say, "you fool, get a towel." Now, though the waiter did not know what *was* the right thing for the service, he knew it could not be *a towel*, for it could never be, that a thing which was considered so great a luxury for the face, could be degraded to the ignoble service of the *feet;* and the idea striking him as ludicrously as his simplicity had Judge C., he commenced laughing at the strange conceit, of what he thought was the Judge's pleasantry, or "funnin'," as he called it; and went down with his chuckling laugh, that "this nigger could'nt be fooled that way; he did'nt know much, but better raised than that,—towel for de foot, yah! yah!! yah!!!—no sich fool as dat, yah! yah!!" And into the kitchen he went, where he was joined in the laugh by cook and other servants; whether at the simplicity of Jim or the "funnin' of the Judge," I know not, but presume it was the latter. The Judge had to go without his foot-towel, but was amply compensated by the laugh, which he relished so heartily.

Judge Cone was the most agreeable circuit companion I ever knew, besides being one of the ablest—if not the ablest—lawyers in the State. He had wit and an inexhaustible humor that made his society, on the circuit, always agreeable.

He once represented his county in the State Senate, when he had several acts passed that were worth more than all the others of the session, and which will, no doubt, stand their ground almost, without amendment, as long as Georgia shall have statutes. In the Senate, as at the Bar, his humor and wit enlivened, very much, that sedate body. The following is an instance of his capacity to make amusement out of any and everything: When one of the candidates for Doorkeeper came to his room, canvassing for his vote, the Judge asked "if he had ever *kept* a door," being answered in the negative, he next asked the aspirant for portal honors, if he had " ever *seen* a door kept," and receiving the same answer, he asked the seeker of votes, if he had " ever read a treastise on doorkeeping," and the answer disclosing that he had never gone through such a preparatory course, to learn the mysterious art of doorkeeping, the Judge told him that he was unfit for such a responsible and difficult office, but if he would get the proper books and study the art, honestly and diligently, for twelve months he should have his vote next year.

Most innkeepers, after a few circuits, learned to have water, clean sheets and scalded bedsteads at the beginning of every court, and clean towels in the rooms, every morning, though I heard of a case in the Cherokee Circuit, not many years since, where a landlady, in the process of learning, declared, that " these lawyers must be a dirty set of fellows, as they will not use the same water and towels after each other, for I can wash my four children in the same water and wipe them with the same towel, and *God knows they are dirty enough.*"

I have noticed that in those portions of the State where cotton was made, the taverns were the worst, because the planters could take no time to do anything else than plant, hoe, plow, pick, gin, pack and haul cotton. No time to feed and take care of stock, and put up the home-comforts, usual in countries were there is some cessation from constant labor at one thing.

CHAPTER III.

Justices Courts.—The Young Lawyer's Toughest Case—A Court broken up in a Row—Deliberation and Impetuosity—Miss Nancy Rumsey and the Irishman—Strange Names of Districts—Wolf Skin—The Lick—Dooley District.

A young friend, formerly practicing law in Wilkes county, Georgia, rising to the dignity of editor of a newspaper, and seeming to have been hard run for matter, wrote the following amusing account of his "toughest law case."

With a hope of aiding him in his extremity, I contributed the three succeeding numbers to his paper; and as they relate to trials in the courts of the Justice of the Peace, in Georgia, they find their appropriate place in this chapter:

OUR TOUGHEST LAW CASE.

The opening of a legal career is usually a probation of severe trial. The "young lawyer" suffers anxieties, secret humiliation and anguish, of which the outside world forms no conception; and for which an after life of success is scarcely a compensation, burdened, as it must be, with constant care and vigilance. In the Superior Courts, indeed, his way is smooth enough, except the troubles which necessarily arise from his own greenness and timidity; for there the presiding Judge will look with indulgence upon his youth, and remembering his own early trials, will carefully refrain from wounding his sensitive pride, and often protect his inexperience from the consequence of blindness or the superior skill of the hardened old brothers; while the latter old fellows themselves, are often disposed to treat him with consideration or even tenderness.

But his natural enemy, is the Justice of the Peace, and especially the country Justice. If opposed before one of these by an old lawyer, "His Honor," in total ignorance of the really difficult questions which often arise before him, always follows implicitly the argument, or rather directions, of the senior advocate, taking it for granted that he knows more about law than the youngster. If unopposed, the old Magistrate is almost sure to decide against the young lawyer, lest the bystanders might think he did not know as much law as the upstart boy, or that he had made His Honor change his opinion; for the harder the head the harder will he hold his point against the hardest logic. Indeed, the case often takes the turn of a fight between the young lawyer and Justice, instead of the plaintiff and defendant.

Every lawyer has had his first experience of this sort. Ours was before a Georgia Justice—and here it is:

A country schoolmaster sued one of his patrons for tuition of two children. The case was first tried before the Justice, without a jury) each party managing his own cause in *propria personæ*. Judgment for defendant. Plaintiff appealed to a jury and came to town and employed us to fight his battle. We had just been admitted to the bar, and on the next Court day of the district, drove out with Stokes, our client, and arrived a little before old Crabman, the Squire. The Court was held in a little log school house, on the roadside, a few hundred yards from the residence of our Justice, who was a country farmer. Very soon we saw him coming down the road on foot, with his negro boy behind him, carrying a jug. The old codger had a fiery red face, rough iron gray hair, and was a self-willed, stormy-tempered man, wearing a green blanket overcoat and yellow plush cap pulled down over his ears. Our client had given mortal offence by appealing from his decision, and it was apparent that we had a hard day before us, when the old fellow passed through the crowd to the door, with a loud "good morning" to everybody but Stokes and the writer, at whom he glanced with angry contempt, as he entered the house. The crowd followed into the room, where the jug was deposited on a table in the centre of the floor, the cob-stopper drawn, and all present invited to take a pull, except poor Stokes and his lawyer, the old Squire concluding the ceremony with a fierce look at us over the jug handle, as the stuff mounted to his nose. Court was then solemnly opened, and ours, the great case of the day, soon reached and the jury sworn. The defendant was no where to be seen, and after proving our claim, and making a modest little speech we sat down and began to anticipate an easy victory, notwithstanding a good deal of annoyance from the Justice when introducing our evidence. But our astonishment was great, when the old fellow, after another turn at the jug, went before the jury and commenced a regular address in favor of the defendant, filled with the most violent abuse of Stokes, and his little "squirt of a town lawyer who came out to teach *him* his business." We jumped up and commenced a protest against a Magistrate taking sides in his own court. The contest grew high and furious, when he ordered us to sit down, or he would make the Constable arrest us for contempt of Court. He then concluded his speech, directing the jury to withdraw and find for the defendant. They went to a neighboring thicket to consider of their verdict while old Crabman and ourself contiued the controversy outside the door, with the trunk of an old sassafras tree between us, upon the soft bark of which we whittled, slashed and bored away with an energy proportioned to our excitement. After about a-half hour spent this way, the Constable came in with a message from the jury, saying they were "hung," and wanted the jug sent out. The jug was sent, but very soon failed to produce unanimity, as in a little while we heard, from the thicket, laughter, songs and quarreling, intermingled with loud discussion of the case. Towards evening the Constable staggered in again, followed by a few straggling jurors, looking as if they had the square-toed measles, to report that "two of them jury fellers has stole off and gone home, some of them is down thar pukin' drunk, and these here, say d—d if they'll stay any longer 'bout this fool business."

Whereupon Squire Crabman declared it a mis-trial, and dared us, if we thought we could beat him in his own court, to come back next session and he would show us. We did not go.

A COURT BROKE UP IN A ROW.
[NO. I.]
BY AN OLD GEORGIA LAWYER.

Mr Editor:—Having lately been much amused by reading your experience in a Justice's Court, I have thought you might be entertained with my troubles in the same jurisdiction.

Some fifty miles above Augusta, Ga., stands the old town of Wrightsboro, so named in honor of the last Colonial Governor, Sir James Wright, of the then province of Georgia. It was noted for the belligerent character of its men and their use of the "Wrightsboro," a knife since called the Bowie.

About forty years ago, returning in the stage coach from Columbia Court, I stopped in this straggling village for dinner; when "big fighting Dave Huff" applied to me to draw him a warrant to arrest Pat Hughes for assaulting him with a crooked stick, which Pat carried many years before and after this memorable occasion. Pretending the importance of my presence at my office—you know young lawyers use such pretences for obvious reasons—I objected to staying over for so small a matter. But as "fighting Dave" promised a big fee, considering the size of his case and counsel, I remained and drew his affidavit and warrant, which was issued by Justice Wright, of the village, and Hughes was arrested. On account of the consequence of the parties—Dave being the bully of all that vicinity, and Pat having been an editor—the court of inquiry was set for the following Saturday, and three associate Justices, Smith, Dorsey and Mark Price Davis, were called in by 'Squire Wright to aid and assist.

To the end that you may understand and appreciate the spirit in which his worship, Justice Wright, did business, it will be well to narrate some of his previous official conduct as reported to me.

A merchant having sued a debtor in his court on an open account, his worship gave judgment for the defendant, when the plaintiff appealed to a jury—for in Georgia such appeal is allowed. On the appeal trial, the merchant employed a young lawyer—one of the "squirts," that you mentioned—to attend before the jury. After the evidence, the "squirt" squirted, and his worship, after liquoring the jury, charged them to go out and find for the defendant, as he had. When the jury had retired, the lawyer remonstrated with him for his peremptory and arbitrary charge, on which the 'Squire replied, "By G—d! you need not make such a fuss about your account, I kill notes in my court sometimes as dead as h—ll!"

On another occasion a horse was levied on and claimed in his court, when he decided that the execution had no lien on it, "because the horse was older than the execution."

A neighboring Justice having sued 'Squire Wright, he went with the Constable to see the writ served, and enjoy the dignity of sueing another magistrate, whereupon 'Squire Wright whipped the plaintiff Justice and his Constable; when the latter departed and walked about a mile without saying a word until he stopped, turned around and faced the plaintiff and said, "'Squire Wright is rather snappish this morning!"

He had the talent of making people hate him with a ravenous appetite; to the extent that, one of his kinsmen who had a lawsuit with him, having "come under conviction" at a camp-meeting, could not "get through" or become converted. A preacher instructing the penitent, told him, among other things, he must love God more than the world, forgive all his enemies and spend the night in bringing his mind to a perfect state of forgiveness towards everybody. The next morning the "seeker" hunted out the preacher and accosting him, said, "Mr. Adams, I have made up my mind to go to Hell, for I cannot forgive Zeke Wright, nor love God better than Sally Horton."

Another case is reported on him, though I have heard it attributed to a different Justice; but as it is just what Wright would have done under the circumstances, I give it. In trying a case, the defendant's lawyer commenced cross-examining plaintiff's witness, when Wright interposed, saying, "Mr. H., you can't examine the plaintiff's witnesses, ef you want to prove anything fetch your own evidence, you can't put the plaintiff to the trouble of hunting up witnesses and bringing them here for you to use. No! no! 'Squire H., I let you know every tub stands on its own bottom in this court." Of course lawyer H., about this time became very nervous and was walking the court yard in an agitated manner, when another lawyer, Mr. D., coming, in it was proposed to leave the question to him—"No," exclaimed H., "it is not worth while to multiply words, for this court are a d—d fool!" and seizing the "d—d fool" by his shaggy foretop, knocked his pig head against the bark of an oak tree by which he was sitting, (for it was out doors, with his back to a rough red-oak,) until he knocked the bark off the tree, which H. declared was a summary and efficient *certiorari*.

I could give several other cases, equally as illustrative of Justice Wright, but will let these suffice.

Saturday came, and with it every man, woman, child, negro and dog in all creation round about, to witness the legal pitch-battle between the great bully and the editor. The accused employed a lawyer of the village, Mr. Petit, who brought nearly a wheel-barrow full of books to the court, which convened about 2 o'clock, on the piazza, or gallery of a grocery, under which there was a deep cellar, co-extensive with the house. I opened the case by stating that the warrant had been issued by the learned Justice Wright, whose known accuracy forbade that any exception should be taken to it. Here that learned Judge struck the table with his clentched fist and said, "I pronounce this a bonum fiddle good warrant, by G—d!" I then proceeded to say that being a court of inquiry only, their worships would have nothing to do except to inquire if there was sufficient suspicion or probability of offence, to bind over the accused to answer to any indictment that might be preferred against him at the next Superior Court of the county. But Petit insisting that they should try the question of guilty or not guilty, the four Justices assumed the duties of a jury as well as judges, and proceeded to traverse the issue in due form. This involved the examination of many witnesses, and about sundown, we had to lay one of the Justices (Smith) out on the wood-pile to cool, and I would have been glad to have placed the learned Justice Wright beside him; but it being *his* court, he felt in honor bound to hold up under the load of whisky with which he was staggering. The Magistrates sat on a fixed bench that ran all around the piazza, with a table about four feet square before them; on one side of which stood Mr. Petit with the accused at his back, on another I stood protected in the rear by big fighting Dave, and on the fourth side stood the Constable, while the whole gallery was crowded with the audience. Night coming on, a tallow candle, stuck in a bottle, occupied the centre of the table, and immediately before the learned Judge lay the old Georgia Justice—too old for you to recollect, I presume, Mr. Editor.

About ten or eleven in the night, I happened to read something that had been decided by the Court of King's Bench; when the learned Justice stopped me, with the question, "What court was that you read 'Squire?" "I read a decision, may it please your worship, made by the Court of King's Bench, the highest court known to criminal jurisprudence." "Well it is not prudence to read it to this court. What book is that you are reading anyhow?" "I read from Lord Hale's Pleas of the crown, may it please your worship, the greatest authority we have on criminal law." "King's Benches courts, and Lord's law books! I should like to know what we fout for ef we are to have Kings' law and Lords' law books; and what the Georgia Justice was made for ef it aint the law in Wrightsboro"—bringing down his hammer fist on the "Georgia Justice." "This here town was named after one of them lords that we run out with his law and law books, and though he was named Wright, I scorn to be kin to him."

At this stage of the case the accused could not help looking across the table over my shoulder at big Dave with a triumphant grin, peculiarly provoking, just at that juncture, to the pheelinks of the bully of Wrightsboro; whereupon he shouted, "you laugh at me you d—d rascal!" and charged over the table, knocking down the candle, and grasping at, but missing, his enemy. The scene had crowded the piazza as full as it would hold of eager spectators, when the weight and commotion being too much for the old sills, they gave way and slid justices, constables, lawyers, suitors and spectators into the cellar below. I climbed out amid the clicking of cocking pistols and the gleaming of the starlight on the blades of the Wrightsboros; and presently followed Dave with a shooting iron in his hand about two feet long in the shape of an old rusty horsemans pistol, poking it against every man he met, shouting he would kill the d—d rascal," until he cleared the yard. I, being his lawyer, was the only one who dared approach him, which I did—in the rear.

And this was the first and last court I ever saw break up in a row.

DELIBERATION AND IMPETUOSITY.
[NO. II.]

It was my good fortune to know—in Wilkes county, many years ago—two very estimable gentlemen, of great hospitality; one, the elder, was known as "gentlemanly Billy Grimes," to distinguish him from another Billy Grimes, of the same county, who was equally estimable, and I don't know that he was not quite as gentlemanly; yet the reasons why one was called gentleman and the other not, will illustrate a subtle distinction which people make in the elements that constitute, or rather constituted, a gentleman—for I am writing of half a century since; of a time when "niggers was niggers," land fresh and rich, and cotton twenty cents a pound.

Gentlemanly Billy wore a nicely brushed beaver, broad, spotless ruffles, broad-cloth coat and polished boots; was a planter; came to town in his carriage; gave dinner parties, and, sometimes, sent his daughters to dancing-school, or rather brought them—for he "loved to see the young people dance"—took a drink with the boys, and was what you might call "an old boy," though not *the* old boy. It was an idea of Bulwer, I believe, that to live a long life, you should associate with old men when young and with young men, when old; and a good idea it was, Mr. Editor, as I could show were I not afraid of boring your readers.

The Billy Grimes who had *not* the complimentary prefix to his name, was a merchant; lived in town; wore seedy clothes—though wealthier than our "gentlemanly" Billy; never associated with young men; never gave dinner parties; was a methodist; went to church every Sunday; hardly ever laughed—a hearty one would have thrown him into convulsions—and would nearly as soon have sent his daughters to a brothel, as a dancing school.

An old negro man of his, gave an opinion of his old master and mistress, after their deaths, in the following words:

"Old master was a mighty strait-paf mefodis—don't know his Christian paf was so strait. Old missus was a strait-paf mefodis, and Christian-paf too, and *she* gone to heaven, but I never hearn where old master stopped at."

Now, this Billy, was as worthy as the first, and though the contrast of their characters has nothing to do with my story, I have drawn it for the purpose of showing something of the constituents of a gentleman fifty years since.

A peculiarity of our friend "gentlemanly Billy," was his slowness and deliberation of speech; for he made a pause of a second or two between every word, besides bringing them "long drawn out." He was never known to be in a hurry or excited; took his time for everything, and Gabriel's last trump would have startled him no more than a dinner-horn. Judge Dooley, of whom I will have much to say in future numbers, if I do not break down, told a story illustrative of this eccentricity. It seems that our gentleman had an acquaintance living in Augusta, not far from the Savannah river, and walking on the banks late one evening, turned off to his friend's house, in an easy walk, and called at the gate, when Mrs. Chapman came to the door, and after the usual salutations, he asked after the health of her family, with one foot on the fence and his arms reposing comfortably on its top, drawling out his sentences with his usual deliberation; and being answered and receiving a similar inquiry, he replied that all at home were well, &c., &c. " Come in! Come in, Mr. Grimes," said Mrs. Chapman. "No—no—I—am—in—a—hurry,—for,—as—I—came—along—the—bank—of—the—river—some—one—was — drowning — and — called — for — help, — so — I—thought—I—would—get—a—light—and—see—if—I—could—not—go—down — and — help — him. Will — you — have — the—kindness—to—furnish—me—a —light?"

Now, there was a Colonel Hartwell, a neighboring planter and country merchant, who was as remarkable for impetuosity and rapidity of utterance as Grimes was for the reverse. He threw into his life such energy, that he died one of the largest cotton planters and richest men of the State. Though of feeble health, he held out to be some sixty years old, because he could not take time to be sick and die before. An anecdote told of him by a kinsman, Col. J——, will illustrate his hurricane-manner of doing business. He had several large plantations in South-western Georgia, on which he had overseers, and upon some of them his sons, with no residences but common log cabins, containing, sometimes, no more than a single room. Being very hospitable, when making a round of visits to his places he would ask everybody he met to go to the plantation, and often, particularly during court weeks, would have his cabins filled like bee-hives, (as I have often witnessed myself).

On one occasion, Col. J—— said he arrived just at dark at one of his single-room villas, and found Hartwell with the overseer's house full of company; looking around, he was thinking to himself, where in the name of wonder, would all these people sleep, when Hartwell commenced asking after friends and relatives, and among the latter, after cousin Betty. Col. J——, to see how the announcement would affect his host, and curious to know to what expedients he would be driven in such an extremity, told him that cousin Betty would soon be there to spend the night; that he had left her carriage not more than a mile back, and rode forward to announce her coming. Hartwell sat silent for a moment, the first time in a week, pondering what was to be done with cousin Betty. Suddenly springing to his feet, he exclaimed, with the rapidity of rain drops falling on a tin roof, "Tom!" (his son,) "Build a house for cousin Betty! Build a house for cousin Betty! Build a house for cousin Betty to sleep in to-night! Henry! D—n it, Henry, cousin Betty must have a house to sleep in to-night!" and running to the door, grasped an axe with which a negro was splitting lightwood knots; dashed open the head of a hound waiting for his supper, knocked down the overseer, whipped two darkies, and got a log cabin nearly half finished before they could stop him."

Grimes and Hartwell were both neighbors, both fond of company and very hospitable, and withal of festive habits, frequently visiting, each at the other's house. Once, during the Christmas holidays, Grimes and several other gentlemen, were spending a day or two at Hartwell's, (who was then a bachelor,) and when playing whist in an upper room, after supper, Grimes came down and said, with the pause of a semicolon between each word, "Colonel Hartwell, we want some water up stairs." Hartwell replied at the rate of a hundred and fifty words to the minute: "Water! water! water! Tom, water! water, up stairs! Have any more refreshments, Mr. Grimes? Toddy! toddy! toddy, more apple toddy, Tom; make the gentlemen up stairs more toddy! toddy! apple toddy, you d—d nigger! apple toddy! Egg-nog, Mr. Grimes? egg-nog, egg-nog, egg-nog, Tom, you stupid nigger! Make the gentlemen some egg-nog, you d—d rascal!" Then galloping through the same formula to whiskey punch, he stopped to cough and catch his breath, when Grimes interposed with all the composure with which he had asked for a light to save the drowning man, and pausing this time a colon between each word, said, "But Colonel Hartwell, there is a fire up stairs ——" when Hartwell broke in at race-horse speed, "More wood! more wood! more wood! Lightwood! lightwood, Tom! you sloth! more lightwood! cart load of lightwood, you slow negro, d—n you! Make a night of it, Mr. Grimes! We will make a night of it! a night of it, sir!" (Here Grimes not knowing how long it would be before he could start again, lighted a cigar, and taking a seat commenced smoking.) "Christmas times, Mr. Grimes! Christmas times, you know," and Grimes would have smoked out his cigar before he could have wedged in another word; but a log of wood rolling down, H. took up the tongs to replace it, and made cessation enough for Grimes to take his weed from his mouth, and blowing out smoke, as he knocked the ashes from the burning end, said, "But Col. Hartwell, the house is on fire!"

Then Hartwell broke in, but as it was impossible to increase the speed of his volubility, he made it up by pitching his voice to the steam-whistle key. "Tom! Peter! Jack! Dick! d—n it! Plows! Hoes! Spades! d—n it! Corn! Fodder!" and so on until he had run through an inventory of his estate, before he could strike water! water! fire! fire!" and then went it strong on that line until he had suppressed the flames, but not before they had burnt a hole through Grimes' bed-room floor, which I have often seen.

Grimes, in the meantime, finished his cigar in his chair, and then went to resume his whist.

There had just been elected a Justice of the Peace, for the District in which the above scene occurred, who had held but one court since his term of office commenced. There were also two waggish young lawyers in the town near by, who knowing the greenness of the new 'Squire, concluded they would make a case out of the affair just related, for the purpose of puzzling him. Getting permission of the parties, one brought a suit in the name of Hartwell against Grimes for slow talking, by means of which his house was burned to the great damage of him, the aforesaid Hartwell, &c., &c. To which Grimes' attorney plead a set off of fast talking by Hartwell, by means of which Grimes could not talk. After discussing the merits and demerits of fast and slow talking; minding your stops, and not minding them, &c., the learned Justice gave his judgment that as Hartwell's fast talking was as bad as Grimes' slow, he should have nothing for the burn, and if Hartwell did not mind his stops better, he would be worse burned next time.

MISS NANCY RUMSEY AND THE IRISHMAN.

[NO. III.]

Mr. Editor:—I will report you but one more case in the Justice's court; and I regret exceedingly that so much valuable legal knowledge must be lost to jurisprudence for want of a more able and industrious reporter. There is a rich mine of legal wealth unexplored in the old cigar boxes and chinks of ancient storehouses at almost every cross-road in Georgia.

When I first attended Elbert Superior Court, almost fifty years ago, I noticed a large woman, "fat, square, and forty," or more, drive up her ox-cart, back it up near the pathway that led to the main door of the Court House, scotch the wheels, unhitch her two oxen, and, with the aid of two friends who came forward, tie and feed them. She then removed the hind gate of her cart and exposed the end of a cidar barrel. Another friend climbed over the wheels and handed out a table, cups, pint and quart pots, a box filled with ginger-bread, and finally, a small bag of chestnuts. You have doubtless, Mr. Editor, seen such travelling restaurants in your day.

How often Miss Nancy Rumsey had repeated that scene in years past, I cannot say; but I know she continued it to a late day as regularly as the Court set, until a lawyer once moved that the minutes be amended by adding, after the words, "Present, the Honorable —— Judge, &c.," the additional words, "and Nancy Rumsey and her two red steers," as she and they had been coming long enough to make it a good custom at common law; for memory of man ran not to the contrary; and the whole county could swear that it had been continued without interruption; had been peaceable, &c.; and he doubted whether any lawful court could be held without them.

By her regular business of a few dollars a day, during courts and other public occasions, she had amassed enough to build a comfortable house some six or eight miles from Elberton, the county town, up in the "chinquapin settlement, called Goshen." This house of hers was the great headquarters of the country round about, and being on the high road she kept a country tavern, at which I have often drawn rein for rest and refreshment, and always found Miss Nancy an obliging and liberal hostess. From a capitalist she became a politician; and the first thing a candidate had to do before entering the canvass, was to subsidize this influential lady. I learned from conversation with several aspirants for public office, that she had taken tribute alike from all. Each got her promise of favor and she got money from each. The candidates soon found this out, but they knew also that if they did not pay this tax to the queen of Goshen, they would get her earnest opposition; and so this white female levied black mail on all office-seekers in Elbert county, for half a century.

For the last twenty years of that period, after her throne had been well established, not only candidates stopped to have a word with Miss Nancy, but the lawyers, who were looking up business, took care to say pleasant things to her as they passed; and the Judge, as he went by, paid his respects as she sat in her chair at the end of her cart.

I have said that the custom of the attendance of Miss Nancy and the oxen had been peaceable; but on one occasion, it came near being disturbed from a source that seems to have been a disturber of all thrones. A late importation from the Green Isle, finding his way to Elberton, and to Miss Nancy's cake cart, bought a mug of cider, but after it was drawn, and before paid for, concluded he would swap it for a ginger-cake; to which she consented and poured the cider back into the barrel. Pat having eaten his cake, started off, when he was called back by the vigilant Nancy, and reminded that he owed for his purchase. "Not paid for the cake!" exclaimed Pat. "Didn't I swap ye the mug of cider for it? and now you want pay too." "But," said Miss Nancy, "you didn't pay for the cider." "Not paid for the cider, is it? Bedad! ye poured it back into your bar'l, where it now is. None of yer thricks, ye Jezebel; none of yer shabby thricks to chate an honest furrener out of his little penny. Mistress Rumsey, ye got yer cider in yer bar'l which I swapt for yer cake, and now to talk of pay for yer cake!" and off he turned indignantly.

Though Miss Nancy could not, in her confusion, unravel Pat's false logic, she could see so far as to know that whereas she had eighteen cakes, she now had but seventeen, and no money for the missing one. She therefore sued Pat, with the hope that the Justice, learned in the law, could explain it. When the suit came on for trial, Pat appeared and arguing the case with the same earnestness and subtlety that he had at the cart, confused the court as much as he had Miss Nancy; but all unconsciously to the confident Justice, who tried it. In giving his opinion, the latter said the case was very plain, though neither of the parties seemed to understand it; and pronounced his judgment that Pat should buy and pay for another cake and swap it back for the mug of cider, to please the plaintiff, who seemed so dissatisfied with her former trade; and she should let Pat drink his cider and he would have the worth of his money—and she the money for her cake, and the worth of her cider in the cake given back, which would make them even.

I would have the reader know that such Justices and judgments as the foregoing, are the exceptions to the generality of that large and worthy body of magistracy known as Justices of the Peace.

The counties of Georgia are divided into Districts of a few hundred inhabitants, each, over which two resident Justices have jurisdiction. The places of holding courts are, generally, called lawgrounds. The names of some of the districts are very quaint—and generally significant of some local event or peculiarity—such as Guinea Nest, Rabbit Trap, Shake Rag, Sugar Tit, Shampagny,

Wolf Skin, The Lick, Dooley, Nigger Foot, the Devil's Half Acre, Hello, Red Bone, &c. By much archæological labor, I have been able to give the origin of the names of some, and for the benefit of history, record the results of my antiquarian researches:

There lived, many years since, in a district in Oglethorpe county, a parcel of dare-devils, who dared and defied public opinion, who were as hard night riders as "Brom Bones and his gang," who would play cards, fight chickens, run horse races, and go to church on Sunday and spend sermon-time in trading horses, swaping knives and such-like sinful amusements, and made no concealment of their wicked ways. They called their sisters Beck, Sall and Suck, and their parents, the old boy and old hoss, old mistress and old gal. Courting, they pinched their sweehearts' ears and cheeks until they squealed; slapped them with vigorous love-licks, that made them grunt; hugged with a bear's grip, and kissed them with ravenous appetites. They always took their liquor "straight," chewed tobacco with the left jaw, and never took any physic except number six and jin cocktails. They could beat a negro at the double-shuffle, cut the pigeon-wing two feet from the floor, and "for pluck," always eat game eggs and red pepper for breakfast, and drank gun-powder tea for supper. They swore they were no wolves in sheep's clothing, that they wore the wolf's skin, because they *were* wolves, and no sheep, and "did not care who know'd it." And they properly gave the name of "Wolf-Skin" to a district which is not now more wolffish than some others having more lamb-like names.

Judge Dooley was once holding court, in the fall, when the people, suffering very much with chills and fever, gave evidence of it in the ghost-like appearance of those in the lobby of the courthouse. The Sheriff, was by law, required to advertise a sale in three of the most public places in the county. He selected the court-house and a place blessed with a mill and grocery in conjunction, and was therefore able, satisfactorily, to comply with two of the conditions, but as he was at a loss where to find the third most public place, the Judge directed him "to put it up at the claybank where all these people go to lick dirt." Now most of the cadaverous crowd coming from a particular district, it went, forever after, by the name of "The Lick."

Warren county was taken from the territory of Wilkes, and an action of ejectment having been brought for a tract of land lying in the former, Dooley was employed as counsel for the defence. When the case came on for trial, the plaintiff made out his chain of title very completely, and Dooley introducing no evidence, the plaintiff's counsel thought his case safe for a recovery. Dooley said, "though he introduced no evidence, he should read and rely on the Act of the Legislature organizing Warren county out of the territory of Wilkes. The lawyer of the plaintiff was puzzled to see what that Act had to do with the case, and ridiculed the forlorn hope of the defendant.

Now, one of the main deeds of the plaintiff having been forged —and attacked on that ground—had to be dated far enough back to be older than the genuine deed of the defendant, and the antedate happening to be before the organization of Warren, it should have been dated in Wilkes, and the land described as lying in that county, but instead it was dated in Warren, and the land described as lying in a county that then had no existence.

Dooley, in making his concluding speech, told the jury "that, two years before there was any Warren county, it seems remarkable the drawer of the deed should have known there would be a new county; more remarkable, that he should have known this land would be in it; and still more wonderful, he should have known it would be named Warren."

The people were so pleased with Dooley's management of his case, they called the district in which the land lay, "Dooley District." And they having been—by said trial—admonished of the danger of knowing things too soon, have gone to the other extreme of not knowing them until long after known everywhere else. Grier's Almanac—at that time the forerunner of all literature in Georgia —had not penetrated the dreary pine forests of Dooley District. So, fearing they might commit the imprudence of prematurity, the citizens would never celebrate the fourth of July until they had "heard it norated about" that it had been honored with the usual festivities in the regions round about; and this generally being about the last of the month, they had that celebrated—rejoicing on the fourth Saturday, instead of the fourth day of July—to the end "there should be no danger of being before their time."

Dooley District, since that time, having been made a new county of, and having court twice a year, and a mail each week, has caught up with its neighbors and surpassed some of them in many important particulars.

CHAPTER IV.

The Northern Circuit.—Leading members of the Northern Bar, half a century since—First Records of Wilkes County—Judge Dooley, his birth, education, habits and talents,—Tom Peter Carnes—He and Dooley practice in South Carolina—Carnes' speech on a sylogism—Charles and the Lawyers at breakfast—Singular treatment of slaves—Dooley's speech on the nuncupative will—A will made at the bottom of a well—Dooley's happy manner of saying things—Corn good enough for his horse—Jolters—Don't let him shoot this way—Comparison between Dooley and Charles the Second—Mr. Sheriff, some more water out of that same well—How Dooley tried to stop gambling—His fight with Long—Tait challenges him—Moves to a tavern, where he will be considered a gentleman—Dooley's interviews with the roast pig—Rivalry between the village taverns, and the discomfiture of the little widow—Dooley gets the laugh on a young lawyer—Dooley and the brass-healed Doctor—How he punishes his neighbor, hunting Mark Bond—Judge Crawford succeeds Dooley—How rapidly he rose in life—His appearance, his character, his greatness and talents—He and the Lawyer who repeated his arguments—His treatment of Clark men—Reply to his Priest-ridden Landlady—Fatal meeting with Van Allen—Characteristic interview with Mr. Dawson—He, Van Allen and Gov. Clark—He brings the first *"ne exeat"* in Georgia—The Defendant and Martin at the Corn Shucking—Gen. Heard and his suit—Phil Alston and his amusing originality –How Heard tried to marry off a militia Captain and drunken dependent, and how he prospered—Speech of old Peter Bennett, the constable.

Forty-eight years ago, when I came to the Bar, Dooley, the greatest wit of his day, was on the bench. "Tom Cobb," the great Senator, who "sent his word through the court house wall at every lick;" Mr. Upson, the most profound lawyer in the State; Mr. Lumpkin—late Chief Justice of the State—the most eloquent orator I ever heard speak; Mr. Gilmer, afterwards Governor of the State, and who, in his fury, foamed and spat over the jury; Mr. Pope, who was the only lawyer in the Circuit, I ever knew, who, having lived to make a fortune, and that in one county, "by picking up every acorn that dropped," as Dooley said of him, retired and enjoyed it for years before his death; Mr. Prince, "a man of infinite jest," and in wit excelled only by Dooley; Duncan G. Campbell, father of the late Associate Justice of the Supreme Court of the United States, of that name, the leader of his political party in the State, of captivating address and courtly manners, (and queenly wife), and an orator withal; Jno. A. Heard, Solicitor General, a shrewd lawyer, who never let a point escape him, a rollicking companion, and making more money at the time, than any lawyer of the circuit, and General J. V. Harris, a fine old gentleman with a fine family, of great wealth and greater hospitality, were the leading members of the Northern bar, and all, not only gone, but their memories almost perished with them. For, of all the people now living in the circuit, not one in ten have ever heard even their names—except Dooley's and Lumpkin's—though in their day, perhaps no other eight men occupied more of public attention in the State than they.

The great and important murder and other cases, in which they were the leading lawyers; the political campaigns in which they were the leaders of their parties; the loud hurrahs elicited by their oratory on the hustings, and the applause that followed their speeches in deliberative assemblies, are all buried in obscurity by the lapse of a few years, and only faintly traced through the twilight of a few fading memories.

Though something, even much, might be said of them all, interesting to Georgia people, and particularly to Georgia lawyers, but little or nothing could, that would be worth telling the general reader.

Nothing encourages me to give the little amusing matters which I can recollect of him, more than the knowledge that Judge Dooley's memory has out-lived all his cotemporaries, though several may have been his equals, and in some respects, his superiors, it all indicates that the popular taste appreciates wit more than any other talent; comedy above tragedy, and laughter above thought.

In adjoining, and even in distant States, many of the best anecdotes you will hear, are credited—and often improperly—to "Judge Dooley, of Georgia," while the names of his cotemporaries are never mentioned, and are, perhaps, unknown.

The first records of the courts, in Wilkes county, Georgia, were made up during the Revolution; and when about its close, seven men were hung at "one killing," on indictments for treason about as long as a man's finger, containing, without any specifications, general charges of treason. In one case the record shows that the accused had been acquitted, and that "Col. Dooley," the prosecuting attorney, on the next day stated he had, since the trial, discovered sufficient evidence to convict him, when a new trial was granted the State, and the criminal was again put on trial and convicted. *

---

* Characteristic of those times, Judge Crawford used to tell of the trial of a Tory in Columbia county, soon after the Revolutionary war, who, in his defense before the Whigs, who were trying him, argued the uselessness and wantonness of sacrificing life then, as the contest was over. To which the Whigs replying that there had been so much blood spilled by the Tories, they must have some more in return, when he naively answered, "if blood was all they wanted, then, why not kill a nigger ?"

This "Col. Dooley," I think, was the father of the witty Judge, who I have heard tell how his father was dragged out of his house by Tories—while the boy was under the bed—and murdered.

He was born in that part of Wilkes county now Lincoln, and near what he called "the dark corner," where he lived and died. He read law with Mr. Matthews, of Washington, Wilkes county, and I have heard him say he was confined much to the privacy of the office because his clothes, while a student, were not such as he cared to exhibit in town. The old people who knew him then, represented him as a "sallow, piney-woods looking lad." He grew up, however, to be a man of ordinary size and proper proportions, except that his legs were too small for his body. He had a large head, with that compact appearance noticed in the portraits of the first Napoleon, with a florid face, and what is usually called a "bottle nose." His eye was his marked feature, brilliantly black and protruding, and by its scintillations always indicated when something good might be expected.

He was admitted to the Bar in 1798, was on the Bench many years, and until he died in 1827, when he was succeeded by Wm. H. Crawford, Secretary of the Treasury during the administration of President Monroe. I never knew him as a lawyer, but his reputation as a debater, among his cotemporaries, was of the highest order. His education was limited and confined to what he had learned at the "old field schools" of the country. Considering his talents, his associations had been grovelling, never caring for ladies' society, but seeking fun and making butts of his companions. He spent his life, before going on the Bench, in social festivity—his native talents placing him at the head of his profession with but little study or labor. After his elevation to the Bench his habits were restrained within the bounds of decency, if not wholly corrected. Indeed, he then had the carriage and habits of a gentleman, and though never drunk on the Bench, he often showed, in the morning, suspicious signs of a night of debauchery. His mind was so discriminating and clear that he made an able Judge, on whom a good argument was never thrown away. He was peevish and impatient, and fastidious of his personal comforts, which made him, on the Bench, unpleasant to the lawyers, and a terror to bad tavern-keepers, when at his quarters. His conversation and wit were so captivating that wherever he was all classes gathered about him to listen.

He would, intuitively, know whom to select as a butt for his amusements, greatly to the entertainment of all listeners.

Besides drinking, he had indulged in gaming; and I heard him say when he relied on his own judgment, and kept sober, he always won.

If ever there was a greater wit in Georgia than Dooley, by reputation, it must have been Tom Peter Carnes. (There were two Carnes—Tom Peter, a Judge in the last century, the uncle, and his nephew, the wit*). He—the wit—and Dooley were cotemporaries, and both lived on the Savannah river, (Dooley in sight of it), and practiced in South Carolina, in the districts bordering on the northeast bank of that stream. Being a couple of rollicking young wits, not much observant of the rules of polished society—especially if they stood in the way of their fun—not dressing or travelling in much style, and, probably, a little rude withal, they were not recognized as members of the brotherhood, by the Carolina gentlemen of the bar, many of whom travelled in carriages with servants, dressed neatly and were too courtly in their manners for the sprightly, careless young hoosiers from the then new and uncultivated State of Georgia. But the two wits had a weapon for revenge that not only turned the Carolinians down, but drove many of the most aristocratic and dignified from the courts of the districts lying contiguous to Georgia, where the two former practiced. Though Dooley's modesty gave the wit of Carnes—which he held in the highest admiration—the credit of the victory, tradition and reputation give him his share in the contest. He used to give us some of Carnes' speeches, when in conclusion on the enemy. I now recollect but one, which ran in this wise : A Carolinian, who had preceded him, arguing very logically, made a syllogism of his case; having his major and minor propositions and consequence following them. Carnes in reply, said, "the gentleman preceding him, had very unnecessarily, and, he thought, unfeelingly introduced the name of a very honest, simple-hearted and inoffensive family, living down on the river, opposite his brother Dooley, in Lincoln, and who could vouch for the integrity and worth of all the Syllygisms. Gentlemen of the jury, that you may judge for yourselves of the animus with which the

---

*Tom Peter Carnes, the elder, was a lawyer of reputation in Maryland, intimate with the family of Mr. Wirt, in Virginia, married his sister Elizabeth, and came to Augusta, in the last century, where he was a lawyer of distinction and Judge of the Superior Courts of this State.

Mr. Wirt was a great favorite of his (and the old people said of much nearer kin than brother in-law) and, when a lad, visited Mr. C., in Augusta.

In the life of Mr. Wirt, Judge Carnes is mentioned by the name of Thomas A. Carnes. But the records of Wilkes court show that, at Augusta, on the 9th of April, 1792, rules of court were made, signed by " T. P. Carnes, John Y. Noel, George Walton and John Houston," as Judges. The Attorneys and Solicitor General were present as the law then required.

gentleman, preceding me, has dragged my inoffensive friends into court, it is material to state that there are two families of the Gisms in this district: one—on account of its character for violence—is called Fire-Gisms, and the other, not because it wants sense, but because of its simplicity and credulousness, and unsuspicous character, is often imposed on, and is, therefore, called Silly-Gism. Now, gentlemen, you can judge of the motive that prompted the gentleman to select the Silly-Gisms, rather than the Fire-Gisms, for exposure in court, though it may not be very creditable to his courage. The old gentleman, old Major Silly-Gism, was so domestic and unobtrusive that he had hardly ever been in a court-house, much less had he ever a suit at law, and if he was to hear his name had been bandied about here, as the gentleman has done, he would not sleep for a week. Indeed, I do not know but the old Major would leave the country, fearing the lawyers might next have him in jail; and the gentleman was not satisfied with draging the Major's name into court, but must also lug in the minor Sillygism. You know, gentlemen, being a minor, he could not sue or be sued, and, therefore, could never have had anything to do with courts or lawyers. I presume he has never been from home, hardly, and is now on the banks of the Savannah at one end of a fishing-rod, alternately nodding and fighting musquitoes, all unconscious how the learned gentleman is so rudely tossing his name about the court-room. But, gentlemen, that is not the worst. The old Major's wrongs were bad, the minor's worse, but what is worst of all, is the cruelty of introducing that poor, little, timid, sweet-sixteen, Miss Consequence Sillygism's name, so heartlessly, in the hearing of all these men. If the poor little dear shall hear of it, she will cry all day, and go snubbing to sleep like a slapped baby. Who would have expected that so learned, dignified, courtly and chivalrous a gentleman, would have so heartlessly used the name of a little, modest, timid country girl, for no other reason than because she had the misfortune, poor child, to be born a Sillygism?

I recollect to have heard Dooley say, that he and Carnes—going the circuit on one occasion—travelled a long distance for breakfast, on their way to a court that they were likely to reach at a late hour, and calling for it in much haste and impatience were told, by their hostess, they should have breakfast as soon as Charles came, when she called Charles, blowed the horn for Charles, and sent for Charles. And when Charles came, instead of being the husband, or some male relative, as they had imagined, he turned out to be a big, very black negro. When she remonstrated with Charles for being slow, as the gentlemen were in great haste to reach court, he answered, that he would take his time, let gentlemen wait, no more gentlemen than he, etc. When they went to the table there was, in the centre, a pewter basin of clabber, surrounded by three pewter spoons and three chunks of corn-bread, one for Dooley, one for Carnes, and one for Charles; when Carnes, taking up his spoon and shaking it at him, said, "Spooney your own side, Charles, d——n you," and they spooned away until breaking through the coagulated mass that separated them, they left Charles the undisputed spooner.

This may seem a strange state of society for the great slave State of South Carolina, but it was nothing very uncommon—especially in the poor districts where slaves were few—to occasionally find a negro, with the influence over a family or an individual, that Charles had over one, who, it seems was, or should have been, his mistress—though Charles' was rather an extreme case I admit.

I recollect one summer, when travelling with my family and two servants in Northeast Georgia, stopping all night at a log cabin, with another family with the same number of servants. In the morning we had a good breakfast, when our hostess and a young woman, seeming to be an unpaid help or friend, waited on us at table. After breakfast, going to the kitchen to light a cigar, I noticed that the remains of our breakfast had been transferred to a table there, and that our servants were attended by the same waiters who had just served their masters and mistresses. They seemed not well to appreciate the relation of master and slave—for there were very few negroes in that portion of the State—and I suppose, they thought as their food would be paid for, the attention was necessary as a consideration for it.

On another occasion, having been requested to call at a house, off the road, near Carrahee mountain, for the accommodation of my host, as I rose from the table, I heard a commotion at the door, I turned and noticed "mine host" was trying to drag my reluctant servant to the table from which I had just risen, when I came to his relief by saying, "never mind Mr. H., Ned would prefer having his dinner in the kitchen;" the prompt reply was, "well, I thought the way to honor the master, was to honor the man." The answer, however, was given with a touch of the brogue that indicated his misconception of propriety may have been due, partly, to his foreign origin.

I said Dooley accused Carnes only with the war of ridicule, and that I thought his modesty prevented the acknowledgment of his own participation in hostilities; and tradition corroborates this suspicion, by having preserved one of his speeches on a similar occasion to that which elicited the one related of Carnes. I have heard the scene described in his speech, located on a *fat old* gentleman of Georgia, but I have no doubt some wag used the Judge's wit to "get the laugh" on his obese old neighbor.

It seems, in one of the Carolina courts, one of the "gowned gentlemen"—for, in those days, the lawyers of Carolina wore the black robe alluded to in a former page—and Dooley were engaged in a case to establish a nuncupative will, which turned on the point whether the testator was in such extremity, when it was made, as would justify a will made without the usual formalities. Dooley having the conclusion, and being opposed to the probate of the will, contended that the testator was not in such *extremis*, as the law required, to dispense with the solemnity of a written will, and proceeded to give the jury such a case as the law contemplated to authorize such extraordinary indulgence to the testator. "Now, gentlemen," said Dooley, "I will give a fair case of a *will* made in *extremis*. I heard the learned gentleman, who has just taken his seat, say, during the court, that he was fattening a very fine steer, which he intended to kill for beef on his return home. Suppose, as soon as he arrives home, feeling ravenous for beef, he should, before disrobing, order his son or servant to take the gun and go out and shoot the aforesaid steer; that the shooter should return, saying, he had shot and only wounded it, and that it had turned on and chased him out of the field. Now, the brave gentleman would, no doubt, pooh! pooh!! at such a cowardly excuse, and seizing the gun, would march, with hasty and martial tread, to the field of blood, as dauntlessly as a Spanish matadore entering the arena—vulgarly called the "bull ring"—and finding, probably, the steer in the shade of a simmon tree, fighting flies with his tail, and shaking his head with defiance, would raise his gun at a respectful distance—I say respectful distance, for though the gallant and learned gentleman may not be afraid of the face of man, he would be excused, gentlemen of the jury, for feeling a little ashamed to look a mad steer too closely in the face—would raise his gun, gentlemen, at a respectful distance and fire. The goaded and infuriated steer putting his nose to the ground, no doubt, would give a bellow, and, having no better manners, would charge the gallant and dignified gentleman who had given offence. What, gentlemen of the jury, could he do but march, and marching, walk Spanish, and walking Spanish, double-quick, and double-quicking—I dislike to put the dignified and learned gentleman in such an unbecoming attitude as running, even in imagination—and double-quicking, run, gentlemen? Now, we will suppose that it is some half mile from the aforesaid simmon tree to the nearest fence (and it is very reasonable to suppose, in such an emergency, the gentleman would make a bee-line for the nearest refuge,) and the steer thundering behind, it is to be supposed the gentleman would accelerate his speed, without much regard to the dignity of his going, and that the rush through the air would blow off his hat and bring the tail of his robe at right-angles with his body—that is, if his body were erect; but it is to be presumed, to aid his flight, his body would be so much bent forward that his tail would be nearly in a line with it. Be that as it may, the gentleman having no time to consider the becomingness of his toilet—generally in such good taste—the said tail would, no doubt, give very offensive flutters—and to the steer in his unamiable mood, challenging flutters—and now we will suppose the pursuer has approached so near the retreating, learned, dignified and gallant gentleman's tail that the former could begin to touch it very significantly with his horns, and to blow his hot breath alarmingly near the wearer, so much so, that he would feel he was near his latter end; and the gentleman being considerate would be expected, very naturally, to think about providing for his family by a disposition of his property; and being a lawyer, would, no doubt, then and there, proceed to bequeath in this wise: (here Dooley caught his breath between every few words, as one would in speaking under such circumstances) "Being of disposing mind and memory, though mighty hard run, I will my home-place and house-servants to my dear wife, Caroline, and divide the balance of my property equally between my children, and tell them I died like a Carolinian; and give them my dying admonition, to always beware of wounded steers." And we will suppose, about this crisis the fleeing testator would reach the fence, and at the same time the steer's horns reach him, as he put his foot on the first rail, and tilting the learned and dignified gentleman in the air, wrong end upwards, would let him fall on his head in a brier-patch on the other side, breaking his neck, stiff as it is. The Coroner, after holding his inquest, could only return the truth, that the deceased came to his death in a brier-patch, by an old brindled steer. And, gentlemen of the jury, when the lamented testator's will might come to be presented for probate, there could be no question but that it had been made in the utmost extremity."

It must have been well worth any person's time and money, to have travelled the circuit with these two brilliant and fun-loving young wits; and it would have been a blessing to posterity to have had more recorded, before so much had been lost by time, of that which I am trying to save by the narration of these, my recollections.

I have another case of a will made "*in extremis*," not reported in any law book—and which is of too much importance not to be preserved—told by Judge D., on his father-in-law, old Mr. H——.

On the night of the 13th Nov., 1833—I believe was the time of "the falling stars"—the obese old planter was lying on his sofa, having a negro woman scratching his head, two children picking his ears, two rubbing his hands and two his feet, when he was startled by one—who had been looking out of the window—exclaiming, "lor! master, something is on fire, see how the coals are flying." Kicking and knocking away the seven attendants—besetting him like ants round a dead worm—he went to the door, and seeing the grand pyrotechnic display, sent the whole seven to call Philips, the overseer, whom, when he came, he ordered to call the negroes, and making him collect four of the strongest, he had himself let down his well, and telling Philips to stand at the mouth to transmit his orders, proceeded, shouting from this lower deep, "Philips, make Tom and Peter get on the gin-house, Sam and Bob on the barn, Joe and Jeff on the corn crib, and make the others carry them water. "Philips!"—"Sir!"—"Have them fodder stacks in the gin-house field caught yet?"—"No sir!"—"Philips, an't the grass-field, on the South hill, all in a blaze?"—"Not yet sir, the fire goes out before coming to the ground."—"Philips, have a bottle of that old peach brandy, in the cellar, sent down—for hot as it is up there, it is mighty cold down here—and give the niggers what they want for it will all be burnt up before day."—"Philips, do you smell any brimstone from the fire?"—"I thought, sir, I did get a whiff of it just now."—"Philips, if any of that fire falls down here and should miss me, it will scald me like a hog in a scalding tub, at least it will parboil the life out of me. Philips, get pen, ink and paper, (after they were brought he proceeded): Philips, can you write on the bench where they set the water-bucket?"— "Yes sir!" (After dictating a short will, Philips said he would have to come up and sign in the presence of witnesses, when he proceeded)—"Philips, what is the state of the fire?"—"Pouring like it was raining ten thousand brush-heaps."—"Can't come up yet, Philips. Philips, have you heard Gabriel's trumpet?"— "Not yet!"—"Well, let me know the first toot you hear, that I may have time to pray a little." (Philips proceeded to tell him that there was no use making a will, no how, for all his property would be burned up, and it would be of no use). "Well, Philips! I forgot that." The old Peach having begun to operate, gave him Dutch courage enough to come up, having first had the wagon-body brought near the well and turned upside down, under which he crawled. Philips proposing to have straw put under the body for him to lie on, he objected, "because it would take fire too easily." But ordering sheepskins and blankets, he gave directions to have himself let down again if the wagon body caught fire, and went into his woollen nest under it. The reaction, from the warmth and soothing qualities of the emptied bottle, wrapped him, with his fears, into forgetfulness until the blessed sun, rising before the sleeper, blotted out all appearance of the falling fire. *That will* was never presented for probate.

At this distance of time I remember but few of Judge Dooley's sayings and doings, many having been lost for want of a chronicler, and therefore, I am the more anxious to record those I remember. Like all wits, things said by him had a raciness given them by his manner, that cannot be transmitted to paper, and would fall flat, even if told by others.

He convulsed his hearers on an occasion of this sort: When we were in the horse-lot, at Hancock court, looking at our horses, the landlord of the tavern was recommending, as good food for horses, the cob ground with the corn, in his corn-mill, which he was then praising; upon which Dooley promptly replied, "never trouble yourself, Mr. S., the corn without the cob is plenty good for my horse." Into this he threw significant meanings, such as you penurious old boniface, you think we are so green that you can put off our horses on a few grains of corn with much cob, but I will let you know you can't catch me with what is about as dry as chaff.

When *coatees* and *bootees* were all the fashion he said of his travel over a bad road, "my sulky gave me a thousand jolts and ten thousand *joltees*."

A murder case having been on trial and turning on the point whether the prisoner was justifiable in shooting, there was much said about his "right to shoot" under the circumstances disclosed by the evidence, and the jury returning a verdict in which they intended to justify the homicide, said, "we, the jury find that the prisoner has a right to shoot." On which Dooley promptly replied, in apparent alarm, "Mister Sheriff, don't let him shoot this way."

I don't know but that James the second of England, with all his notions of Divine right, made a better King than his brother, Charles, with all his unprincipled dissoluteness; yet the former had to abdicate in two or three years, while the latter died a monarch in secure possession of the throne, after a reign of twenty-five. The one was the austere bigot, the other the witty, merry, though corrupt, monarch. The former did bad, and said no good things, the latter did as badly, if not worse, but his misdeeds were forgotten in the good humor in which he put the nation by his wit and pleasantness. He "never did a wise thing nor said a foolish one," and what was more important, said many pleasant and witty ones.

If he took bribes from Louis, it was almost forgiven when he said to his brother, then Duke of York, "no one will ever assassinate me to make you King." If the palace was a hot bed of debauchery, it was, as a set-off, the abode of a merry, good humored and pleasant monarch.

Like Charles the second, Dooley could not only say good things to set off his bad deeds, but, what was more fortunate, could say them of the deeds themselves, and always thus gild the pills of impropriety which he administered to the public.

When up almost all night trying Holderness, the Sheriff voluntarily placed a small pitcher on the bench, half filled with toddy, and when it was finished he told that officer to "bring him some more water out of that same well."

When he went to Buck Walker's faro table and broke the bank, during Wilkes court, after having eloquently charged the Grand Jury against the vice and crime of gaming, he excused himself by saying, that finding he could not suppress it by the juries, he had to take that method to do it himself.

When at the bar, Col. Dick Long got the better of him in a stick-fight, and he told the former, he need not be so proud of the victory, for it was no great thing, as he had fought through six States and had never yet found any one he could whip.

When Mr. Tait, with a wooden leg, challenged him, his reply was, he could not fight Mr. Tait, as they would not be on an equality unless he, Dooley, could be permitted to put one leg in a bee-gum; and on being told that he would be published as a coward, said he "preferred filling two newspapers to one coffin."

I have said Dooley was very fastidious about his quarters and a great terror to landlords. Mrs. Dooley being a notable housekeeper, as well as a devoted wife, had indulged his squeamishness about his personal comforts, so much, that it was very difficult to please him, especially if in a petulant mood, as he often was. During his presidency on the Bench, the Augusta bar practiced in Warren court, and, usually, came with equipages, servants, &c., in a style that he thought savored of ostentation; and his jealousy was provoked on account of their receiving (as he thought) more than their share of attention from the landlord.

One morning it was noticed he came from Mrs. Chapman's instead of Parris' tavern, where he had been staying the first days of the court. Some one inquiring what was the matter, he said, he had gone to a place where he hoped he would be considered a gentleman, "for," said he, "I went to the horse-lot, and seeing my horse in the rain, I inquired why he was not stabled, and was told by the hostler that the stable was "full of *gentlemen's* horses, *sah!*" "I made the same inquiry about my sulky, which I found exposed to the weather, and received the reply that the carriage-house was "full of *gentlemens'* carriages, sah." "I asked for a glass in my room and was told that the looking-glasses were all in the *gentlemen's* rooms, sah!" and when I asked for any necessary article, I received the same reply, "all in the gentlemens' rooms, sah," "and saying I would go where I would be considered a gentleman too, I went to Mrs. Chapman's where I hope to sustain that character."

A very pretentious landlord, keeping a "*very* common hotel," was always going to have great improvements to his house, table and furniture. After many false promises of the kind, at last a court came when he redeemed them all by a dish of which any boniface in the land might—as he thought—feel proud. When dinner came, on the first day of court, our landlord stationed himself in the dining-room with a look of unusual complacency; and *Mrs.* landlord with the widow (hereafter mentioned), could be seen peeping through the door leading to her room—the shutter of which was left ajar, for the purpose. The servants seemed unusually polite and active, and three little tow-headed urchins had squatted in the room, with mouths watering, at snuffing the odor of the viands, and seeing the good things at the table. When we came to the table it was all explained by a ferocious looking—though dead—pig, stuffed to bursting, and fuller of light-bread, onions and other condiments, than he had ever been of corn while living; standing erect as life, supported by flankings of Irish potatoes and other props; with tail curled up as the tails of all well-to-do pigs should be; ears erect, as if ready to do battle; with a big red apple in his mouth, as if just stolen from a neighbor's orchard; and with eyes looking the Judge as fiercely in the face as eyes with no "speculation" could look at such a dignitary. Pigee faced the Judge unabashed, and the Judge faced the pig with a quizzical leer. There lay the carving-knife and fork, and there sat the Judge and lawyers all around the table. Whether, because the pig looked so life-like that they feared he would squeal with pain or turn to fight in anger when the fork might enter his flesh, or because they did not know how to begin so great a job as anatomizing so formidable-looking an animal, I will not pretend to say, but none had the boldness to assault the dead pig, so formidable was his attitude. Dinner ended with the pig as whole as when we sat down. Supper came, and the pig came and went, as at dinner, to the confusion of landlord and household, and greatly to the vexation of the tow-heads, who, before that time, expected to have been deep into the stuffing. The same scene was repeated at the three meals next day. The second morning, when the Judge came to the table, there was pigee standing his ground as resolutely and fierce-looking as ever; when, making a bow, the Judge said, "good morning, sir, I am afraid you have lost your appetite, seeing you have not eaten that apple yet, and I presume you are tired attending court. Mr. Sheriff, you may discharge him, on his own recognizance, until court in course, seeing we will have no further use for him this session;" all to the great mortification of the poor landlord, and to the great gratification of the aforesaid tow-heads, who, for one time, no doubt, had their fill of stuffing.

There had been a little by-play going on, behind the scenes, of which the Judge was ignorant, that added much to the landlord's mortification, and which was in this wise: Our landlord, of the pig-tavern, had—like all village taverns in the days of which I am writing—a rival in the turkey-tavern, just across the street. Both had arrived at the advanced stage of the art which required clean towels and water each morning of court week, besides scalding bedsteads just before the sessions. For the court being an important time "for custom," and the lawyers and judges paying promptly and liberally, every preparation was made for the important occasion.

In preparing for the court at which the above pig scene occurred, the war had waged quite warm without much advantage on either side, except that Mrs. Pig had become the envied owner of a-half dozen silver tea-spoons, the thermometer by which she measured the estimation in which her guests were held; the Judge always getting the first silver-spoon in his cup, and the next five, most highly esteemed guests, distinguished by the remainder.

As the time for holding the court approached, the war between the two village taverns had become so fierce as to threaten the bankruptcy of both. For, not to be behind, Mrs. Turkey had gotten six silver tea-spoons, "so called," too; when the Pigs, hearing of the rise, bought six apparently silver table-spoons; and the Turkeys, not being able to equal such extravagance, went and bought a loaf of sugar, which coming to the ears of the Pigs, they, thinking it ruinous to continue the race "on this line," concluded to call in a re-inforcement in the way of counsel.

Now, there was in the county a widow Parkins, who, though husbandless, homeless and childless, had such energy, spirit and address, that they had made her very useful in all domestic emergencies, especially on wedding and other festive occasions, by officiating at which, she had become learned in the fashions. For she knew the most approved style for writing tickets of invitation; how to ice and dress cakes; how guests should be received, and how introduced; how the chairs and lights should be arranged; how the daughters should dress their hair, the mother wear her cap, and how the father—when any one dared say, *how*, to him —should wear his collar and cravat.

"Born before nerves came in fashion," and before it was fashionable for *the sex* to faint at sight of an old ruminating cow, or squeal at the buzz of a beetle, she was often sent for to protect a household of females—called keeping them company—while their male protector might be absent. And though she went to protect, she remained to frighten; for having a large collection of ghost and murder stories, the temptation to tell and hear was so great, that the evenings were generally spent in telling of, and listening to them, though the penalty was to make them all sleep in the same room, and, by dovetailing, in the same bed, if not over five; and that, after an examination of the closets, clothes press, big chest and trunk, to see if no sly ghost or murderer might not be ensconsed therein, besides looking—with trembling and fear—under the bed, and shaking the curtains and dresses hanging in the room, to detect such lurking goblins as might have escaped notice.

Our widow had lately been in an adjoining county as mistress of ceremonies at the wedding of Lucy Swanton, the belle of all the region round about that part of the county in which she lived. So, with her shrewdness, her activity and address, her knowledge of the fashions and of "quality doins," her late observations at Lucy Swanton's wedding, and her ghost stories and gossip, generally, it was decided, by the Pigs, that the widow should be sent for. Accordingly the oldest tow-head was dispatched with a conveyance and suitable ropes and straps to bring her, her band-boxes, carpet bags and trunks—for she carried all her worldly goods with her, not knowing to what vicinity she might next be called.

I have spoken above of the widow's gossip, and protest that no one shall suppose I have done so with the contempt with which that word is usually uttered. Every one loves gossip, and would and should retail it if they have the precious commodity. It is only such people as our widow, who travel about and sojourn in different neighborhoods and families, that can gather it, and it would be very unamiable not to distribute the precious article to eager listeners; besides, it makes their company acceptable, and it is praiseworthy and prudent to make themselves agreeable. And there is as great ingratitude to traduce those who gather and retail it to the great enjoyment of their friends, as there is insincerity in pretending not to like it.

On the arrival of our little widow—for she was rather small, but sinewy and wiry—after ascertaining the contest had extended to buying silver table-spoons on one side and a loaf of white sugar on the other, before making another move it was decided, in a council of war, held by her, Mrs. Pig and the oldest tow-head, that the enemy's camp should be reconnoitered at as early a time as possible. So, Winny, the cook, was sent, as a spy, to the kitchen of the Turkeys, "to pump" Betty, cook for the latter. As soon as supper was over, the night after the arrival of the widow, Winny soon learned from her unsuspecting sister of the pot-hooks, that they would have for court not only apple and peach pies, but custard, "*sarves*," cake and, to crown all, a large stuffed gobbler, and that the white folks were busily engaged in making up something in the house, the name of which she had not heard. Upon hearing this report, the widow determined to ascertain what that nameless something might be, and as the two landladies were hardly on speaking terms, but "measured distances" when they met, like two hens anxious to keep their broods separate, she determined to go, as a spy, to the enemy's castle, to try the virtue of her address and tact. So taking off her workaday apron, and fitting herself with a neat black silk one, fancifully trimmed, she went, the day after the report, with her scissors suspended to her apron string to give herself a smart business air—which she had in an eminent degree without the aid of scissors—and called to see Mrs. Turkey, with the ease and assurance of one who had never seen Mrs. Pig, much less of one who was her ally. Before the usual salutations were over, her hawk-eye spied some new looking goods, on which Mrs. T. and daughter had just been working, and not making out satisfactorily what it was, soon took occasion to say, "that is beautiful goods you have, where did you buy it?" stepping forward to examine, apparently, the quality of the goods, but really the articles into which it was about to be manufactured, and ascertaining that they were curtains, she made her visit as short as delicacy would permit. Returning home, she directed that loaf sugar and some red stuff, suitable for curtains, must be had before night. The landlord of the pig-tavern, by promising the first money that might be received during court, obtained these important materials for the campaign then in its crisis. Before the next morning, our widow had red curtains flaming at the *front* windows of the Pig tavern, though they had to be taken down next night and hemmed—for she considered it important to show curtains first, that they might not be charged with aping the Turkeys. Having trumped that card, she made short work of the tarts and pies, by making "such as they had at Lucy Swanton's wedding, which would be much superior to any that could be produced across the street, by old Betty and the Turkeys to help." As to the cake, all she had to do, was to ice and dress it as "at Lucy Swanton's wedding," and she knew the cake of the Turkeyites would be turned down. And now, the crowning triumph was to beat the gobbler, which could be done by what she had learned at the great and inexhaustible wedding.

They had prepared a pig to be quartered and eaten in that way during court, but as something had to be done to beat the turkey, it was presented in the inviting shape described above. Now the day seemed carried in favor of the Pigs, for who could have divined the mishap, that at the last hour—as in other battles— turned the tide of victory. Perhaps if the Judge could have glanced behind the scenes he would have relented in favor of the Pigs and their ally, the widow, and spared them the valedictory to the pig; and then, again, considering with what a high hand they were waging war on the Turkeyites, one's sympathies may well be with the latter. The Turkeyites, of course, did not fail to say, "pride must have a fall; pride goeth before destruction, and a haughty spirit before a fall, etc." The little widow gladly flew with band-boxes and trunks from the scene of her discomfiture on the first wedding that gave her a chance.

Holding court in July, Judge Dooley, on several occasions, complained of a young lawyer as unusually slow in his business, wanting in his usual promptitude in announcing his readiness for trial, etc. One evening, after adjournment, they, with others, were asked to an office some twenty steps from the court-house to eat watermelons, the weather being very warm, they were kept in a cellar under the latter building, and the slow lawyer proposing to bring another, after eating all in the office, Dooley objected, saying, "no! no!! A., it will get too ripe before you come back."

Forty and fifty years ago all the young medical students of Georgia attended the college in Philadelphia, and on their return brought the latest fashions in dress. If a young man in the neighborhood was about to buy a new coat, he would wait until the young doctors returned, to see in what style it should be cut and made. Now it so happened that Dooley—who had great contempt for, and impatience with all kinds of ostentation and foppery—was taken sick in Milledgeville, soon after the return of a new flock of young doctors, who had settled over the country, and who, this time, had brought brass-heeled boots as the latest foot sensation. Dooley, when in health, was very nervous, and excruciatingly so when sick; and it was his misfortune to have, as a physician, on this occasion, one of the new importation of doctors, brazenly shod, and to have a room at the head of the tavern stairs where he could hear the "sounding brass" ring on every step from the bottom to the top. The young gentleman, seemingly anxious to let it be known, by such annunciations, that he was heel-clad according to the latest fashion, trod with emphasis on every step in his ascent to his patient's room. At the second visit, Dooley's nerves, responding to every tramp, as the doctor came up to his door, he exclaimed, in anger and agony, "*ride* in Doctor."

The Judge lived on a very large plantation on the Savannah river, with hardly a tree within a mile of his house, and said he thought a free circulation of the air was better than the shade trees which would obstruct it. The public road ran in a lane, some mile long, within some hundred and fifty yards of his house, and from which a gate opened to give access to it. About one o'clock, P. M., on a very hot day, some one, instead of opening the gate and riding to the house, stopped, on horseback, at it, and called with such determination to be heard and attended to, that Dooley, who happened to be in his portico on that side of the house, walked down to the traveller, who seemed in such distress ; but instead of a traveller it was one of his neighbors, who asked if he had seen anything of Mark Bond—another neighbor—and, on being answered in the negative, said, "I thought he might have been here," and rode away. The Judge, returning through the hot sun to the porch, not in a very amiable mood, stood watching the offender, as he rode up the long lane as far as he dared, not to let him get out of hearing, and then commenced calling and waiving his handkerchief, until thinking Mark Bond or some other great event had arrived, the neighbor rode back, not only to the gate, but, as Dooley kept calling, up to the portico on which he stood, when he said, "No, I hav'nt seen Mark Bond and I don't care if I never see him again, that's all, you may go now," and turning on his heel, walked into the house, slamming the door behind him.

After the death of Judge Dooley, in eighteen hundred and twenty-seven, or eight, William H. Crawford—of national reputation—was appointed Judge by Gov. Troup.

Judge Crawford was born in 1772, admitted to the Bar in 1798, settled in Oglethorpe in 1799, was one of the compilers of Marbury & Crawford's Digest, in 1802, and elected to the United States Senate in 1807 ; showing a most extraordinary rise in public estimation for so short a time, without noticing his subsequent Secretaryship of the Treasury, under Mr. Monroe, and candidacy —as the nominee of a large and respectable party—for the Presidency in 1824.

When he came on the Bench he was so impaired, mentally and physicially, by bad health, that he was but the wreck of what he had been, so much so, that I doubt doing justice to the memory of so great a man whom I never knew in his prime.

He was the largest man I ever saw to have been so well proportioned, and his face and head indicated a brain of the highest order, as it no doubt was, when in full health.

His greatness was manifested, not only by his talents, but by his stoicism, (I know not what else to call it,) by an indifference to all ostentation, and a disregard of mere effect. He never did anything with a view as to what might be thought or said of it. He was entirely above all the weaknesses—vanity, envy and such like contemptible passions, except prejudice—which the rest of mankind are more or less heir to.

If he made a speech he thought nothing of the manner of delivery, if he wrote he thought nothing of the style, save to express his ideas clearly. He cared nothing to please, if he could convince. So, in society, he cared nothing for its conventionalities—not because he felt above or below them, but because he was so concerned about the practical, that he cared not to think of such matters; and after I knew him he carried it to such an extent that he seemed to be wanting, sometimes, in delicacy. I say *seemed*, for he never designed to hurt the feelings of any one, but taking it for granted that all were as practical as himself, it did not occur to him that the sensibilities of others would suffer by the truth.

To a lawyer, who had repeated his argument until the Judge becoming bored, impatiently exclaimed, " Mr. C., you go round, and round, and round like a blind horse in a gin."

Clark and the Clark party having been his life-long political opponents, he never spared them—thinking that thereby he was honestly doing God and the country service—not understanding how delicacy should stand in the way of such a laudable object.

Once, at Lincoln court, a witness was sworn, whose evidence was the subject of not very complimentary remarks at the dinner-table, where two Clark men were present. Upon some one saying that the witness was an old Clark man, the Judge replied, " I thought so, I thought so."

George A. Young—now of Mississippi, as remarkable for his refinement, consideration and delicacy as the Judge was for the want of them—said, to shield the two at the table, "there were some very good and clever Clark men," when the Judge promptly replied, " mighty few, mighty few, mighty few."

Holding a two weeks' session of Wilkes court, he remained at his tavern on Sunday, without going to church. At dinner his landlady chiding him for it, said, " Mr. H. had preached a mighty good sermon," when the Judge replied, "Mrs. A., I presume you are like my mother, who would go to church and hear the veriest jackass preach and say, 'a mighty good sermon, a mighty good sermon.'"

His great bravery was not without stoicism, for he went on the field, when he killed Van Allen, with a pair of old pistols of Mr. Pain's that he had never tried until the morning that he fought, and then, in trying them, they snapped twice. He would speak of the fatal meeting with as much indifference, as of any common event of his life. I have heard him say that he would have hit his antagonist the first fire but for an ugly face which he made, that disconcerted him, but on the second fire he drew down his hat-brim so that he could not see it, when he "hit him without difficulty."

Mr. Dawson, some thirty years after the fatal event, meeting Judge Crawford, remarked that he had seen Van Allen a few days since. "No," said the Judge, "I reckon not." "But," said Dawson, "I did!" I know him well.

"Don't care how well you may have known him, I know you did not see him."

"Why," said Dawson, "I met him in the Lexington road, got out of my sulky and talked with him."

Crawford, unmoved and composed, replied, "Don't care, Mr. Dawson if you did get out of your sulky on the Lexington road, Van Allen want there, for he has not been seen on this earth for thirty years."

"What," said Dawson, "did I say? why, it was Beverly Allen I saw."

"Very probably you saw Beverly Allen, but I know it could not have been Van Allen." And all with as much indifference as if speaking of any one else. I would not have the reader infer that Judge Crawford was unfeeling, for touch him on the right chord and he was as tender-hearted as a woman. I have often seen him moved to tears by the eloquence of our late Chief Justice Lumpkin.

Van Allen was a cousin of President Van Buren—says Gov. Gilmer in his "Georgians"—and was then Attorney General of the State. With him and Mr. Crawford began the parties, in Georgia, which, for so many years, divided and distracted the people of the State, involving, comparatively, no principle. They received a new impulse of violence when Clark and Crawford fought in the then Indian country, beyond the Apalachee. Van Allen and Crawford having fought at Fort Charlotte, an old duelling ground in South Carolina, below the junction of Broad and Savannah rivers.

I have always thought that Mr. Crawford and Gen. Clark were the leaders, because the champions, not to say bullies of their parties—if we could apply such a term to gentlemen of this standing—as much as from any principle that may have been involved.

Mr. Crawford must have been a very successful lawyer, for I have heard him say he never brought a case in which he did not succeed in obtaining a verdict. Perhaps he may have qualified the declaration by adding, in such cases as those where the evidence proved to be what it was reported when he brought the case. I have heard him say he drew the first "*ne exeat*" that was brought in the State. The defendant, he said, was arrested and brought by the Bowling Green, in Oglethorpe county, after night, where there chanced to be a "corn-shucking."

It so happened that a man by the name of Martin—said the Judge—was at the same place, who having been arrested under a *Ca. Sa.*, had, just previously, gone through the Insolvent Court, and, on account of his frauds, with much difficulty. He was very solicitous to know the process under which the Sheriff—who had stopped to take a drink—had arrested his prisoner, but the name was too hard for the remembrance of the defendant, all he could say, was, that it was "some d——d out-landish name that he could not recollect." Martin eagerly asked if it was a "*Ka-Shaw*," no, said the prisoner, it is a heap worse thing than a "*Ka-Shaw*."

"Well, then," advised Martin, "you had best give up, for *it* turned me down, and I am as near law-proof as any one. Can't be anything worse than a "*Ka-Shaw*." Taking him all in all, when in his prime, Judge Crawford must, I think, have been the greatest Georgian of all.

I have said that the political parties which so long distracted Georgia, began with Crawford and Van Allen. From what was said by Gen. J. V. Harris, then a lawyer of Elbert, it seems it had an earlier beginning.

When I first visited Elbert court—some 45 years since—I saw an old gentleman, hardly decently clad, come to the court-house door in his carriage. A servant carried his split-bottomed chair and pillow inside the bar, then helped his master in, who—by permission of the Judge—with cotton night-cap and broad-brimmed hat on and papers in hand, took his seat. This was "old George Cook," a lawyer who clung to the profession with such tenacity that he continued to practice under such difficulties. Not able to stand, or hardly speak intelligibly, he would get some of the young lawyers to do it for him, after giving them the points.

I don't know but the old lawyer acted wisely, for I think life would have had but little interest for him outside the profession. Mr. Cook had been a Constable in the village of Elberton, then a collecting agent, and finally a lawyer.

Mr. Tait, who was a friend of Mr. Crawford's, had been his tutor, and principal in the academy in Augusta when he (Mr. C.) was his usher, and was a lawyer in the same village with Cook. The two lawyers—said Gen. H.—corresponded by note very freely, particularly Tait, when in the blues, as he often was; and the cunning Cook preserved all the notes of his friend.

In the course of time, Tait, as attorney, had to rule Cook for money collected and not paid over to his client. The latter employed Van Allen, who managed to read Tait's notes in court, and, being a wit and satirist, made much amusement for the loby, greatly to the mortification of Tait. And thus "the fray began," which lasted for quite half a century.

I once read a pamphlet, by Gov. Clark, with some such title as "A Legacy for my Children," and which I apprehend is extinct, for I have often since, fruitlessly searched and inquired for it. From what I remember of its contents, and from what I have heard from those who were cotemporaneous with the events, I think the following may be relied on as elements in generating the Clark and Crawford, and afterwards, Clark and Troup parties in Georgia.

A man by the name of Clary—accused as a horse-thief—was arrested in Greene county and carried before Judge Tait—I presume for inquiry—and who (Clary) charged Gen. Clark with complicity. Mr. Crawford, I think, was attorney for the prosecution. Whatever faults Gen. Clark may have had he was entirely above the suspicion of anything so disgraceful. I think the meeting between Clark and Crawford grew out of this affair. It is proper to say that Clark accused the Judge and lawyer with instigating Clary to make the charge.

I will let Luke Turner, as reliable man as ever lived, who died in Wilkes a few years since, give his account of Clark's redress on Tait.

He said to me, a few years before his death, "I am the only man living who saw the assault of Gen. Clark on Judge Tait. I was standing at the door of my boarding-house, on Jefferson street, (I think was its name,) in Milledgeville, when I saw Judge Tait pass in his sulky (the Judge had a wooden leg). A short distance behind I saw Gen. Clark cantering easily up on a fine sorrel horse, (he always rode a fine horse) and as he passed Tait he threw the lash of his horse-whip across the shoulders of the latter, two or three times."

Judge Eearly fined Clark some two thousand Dollars, which, I believe, was afterwards remitted. Besides all this, there was some sharp rivalship between Tait and Judge Griffin—brother-in-law of Clark—for the Judgeship of the circuit.

Judge Crawford was United States Minister to France during "the hundred days," and when the allies entered Paris. It was said he attracted the special attention of Napoleon, and supposed to be, on account of his strong practical sense, unassuming and unaffected manners and commanding person.

Judge C. used to be very interesting in conversation about this eventful period of French history. I only remember that he said, the terrible Cossacks rode miserably shaggy little ponies, and that the signs of Paris would change in a few hours to suit the changing politics of the hour.

As much as might be said of the bar of the Northern Circuit—for a long time the strongest in Georgia—which might interest the profession of the State, I think of nothing likely to amuse the general reader, unless it be some notice of Gen. Jno. A. Heard and suit, of Elbert, and who was one of Judge Dooley's solicitors a half century since.

Gen. H., for quickness and discrimination, had a mind very much after the pattern of Dooley's, well adapted to sharp practice —more indulged in by lawyers then than now, and not thought unprofessional—and rather admired, if not favored by that Judge.

For one who studied but little, Gen. H. was a very able lawyer, and for years one of the most successful in the circuit, so much so that he made more money at one time than he had any use for as a bachelor. Being liberal, of convivial habits, jovial, and fond of society of that character, he kept open house in Elberton for several years, in which he collected about him a few dependants for butts, and a few gentlemen fond of such life for companions, and all, whether dependants or companions, original characters. One of the latter was Col. Alston—called by his companions, "Phil Alston"—to whose original turn of mind was added a most titillating impediment of speech. I recollect when I was first introduced to him he was just from the court of his county, the presiding Judge of which he very much disliked, and soon he opened on him in this style: (The reader's imagination must supply his laugh-provoking stammer) "Have you got a free negro in your county whose crimes are recorded on his back, that I may hire him to hate him? I never intended to marry, but now I shall, that I may have children to hate his children." Seasoning, as he went on, his "high pitched" language with very originial oaths.

I saw him once in court, when the name of Huey McQuerter—which struck him as a very comical name—was called, rise suddenly, and watch for the representative of such a queer sound. Huey entered, and looked more queer than his name sounded, when Alston stammered out, "Yes! yes!! if I had met him in the road, I would have said, how do you do, how do you do, Huey McQuerter?"

On one occasion, when he had agreed with a client—who was as moneyless as himself—to take his case for one hundred dollars, the former requested him to write a note for his signature, but noticing that his lawyer was writing one for fifty instead of one hundred dollars, he asked the reason, when Alston replied, "I am too poor to loose a hundred, but might stand the loss of fifty dollars."*

Alston was a violent partizan of Troup politics, and was in Milledgeville at the opening of the Legislature, in twenty-four or five, when the Clark party, largely in the majority in that body, were celebrating their victory by a dinner at Buffington's tavern. Coming within the sound of the victor's rejoicings over the festive board, he exclaimed, with his usual stammering vehemence: "Oh! if I was death on the pale horse I would ride rough-shod over that den, recking with infamy, when hell should reap a richer harvest than at the destruction of Sodom and Gomorrah."

If a fight was accessible he generally had a part in it, and on an occasion of a riot, he was called in court as a witness, and giving in his evidence, said, "some one made a noise like that of a cock, not true game, when struck with the gaff."

The Judge asking what kind of noise that was, he answered, "he would let his Honor hear it," and clearing his throat commenced the stricken-croak before the Judge could stop him.

He was very thriftless, so much so, that going on a hunting excursion, in the new county of Gwinnett—in which he first opened his office—he remained out over return-day, when clients left with his landlord forty notes for him to sue, besides those taken away. As may well be supposed, he had very little of that of which Gen. Heard had an abundance; and whose open house and purse were as acceptable to the former, as his wit and jovial temper were to the latter.

He made one of Heard's butts—a Scotch schoolmaster—shoot his own horse, by having painted in his forehead a white star, looking like another horse that had trespassed on the pedagogeu's barley lot. Another, one Capt. Ragsdale, becoming stupid and troublesome on account of too frequent visits to his sideboard, the General

---

* I have heard this anecdote credited to Sam Flournoy, as well as to Alston, but it is so much like the latter that he would have said it under the circumstances, if he did not.

concluded to dispose of by marrying him off to some woman who might be fool enough to take charge of him, and to aid the suit and please a fancy of the Captain's, Heard loaned him his horses, barouche, driver and part of his wardrobe, to visit the Miss Morton's, of Abbeville District, South Carolina, just across the Savannah river. The terms of the loan were, that the Captain was not to touch a drop of spirits before his return.

Mr. Morton and his family were "very nice people," and entirely too decent for such a debauchee to visit. He, however, was received politely, and treated hospitably. Mr. Morton was a planter, owning a blacksmith shop and country store, and, as was the custom then, kept spirits always on his sideboard, and withal was an active business man. In the morning after the arrival of the Captain, when he came down, Mr. M. invited him to the sideboard.

"No! No! Oh, no! Mr. Morton, I have not touched a drop in twenty years, never could bear it. One of my great objections to visiting our agreeable friend, Gen. Heard, of whom we were speaking last night, is the drinking habits that some of his guests indulge in. It have threatened several times not to visit him at all, unless he ruled his household better, but some how when I get in my carriage, John and the horses will turn their heads that way, and no wonder, for it is a pleasant place enough for horses, servants and convivial young men."

"Well," said, Mr. M., "there are books and the latest papers, amuse yourself as best you can, until the ladies come down, I am obliged to see after some business before breakfast."

As soon as Mr. M. had left the house, and everything seemed quiet, and the decanters shining ivitingly with their brilliant and tempting contents, the thirsty Captain—on a twenty-four hour's abstinence—concluded he could take a drink without discovery, and apprehending he would have an opportunity but for one, took what would have been considered a double dose, at even Gen. H.'s much abused sideboard. Happening to take his draught from a bottle of mellow old peach, of which he was particularly fond, it aggravated his thirst so much that he snatched another, a match for the first. Seating himself to read, he accidently found something so interesting that he read on until the narcotic effects of the "old peach" had weakened the hinges of his jaw, so that the door, through which it had just gone down, dropped half open and the end of his loosened tongue was peeping out of its prison. The neck having become too weak and limber to support a head, filld with leaden dullness, the latter had dropped forward so as to bring his protruding tongue in a situation to distill exuding drops of low-wines on Gen. Heard's black cassimere pantaloons. Too unconscious to protect himself, all the flies in that part of creation seemed to have collected about him, as if he had been. Pharaoh amidst the grevious swarms brought on him for the benefit of the children of Israel.

While in this interesting attitude, Miss Susan, all curled and sweetened up, frisked into this gallant Militia Captain's presence, announcing herself, chirpingly—before fully noticing the predicament of the object addressed—with a "good morning, Captain Ragsdale." The stimulating effects of the damsel's musical and ringing voice strengthened the neck and eyelids of the drowsy gallant so much, that, by their combined efforts, she was brought within the field of vision of his upturned eyes, and mistily peering through the flies that swarmed in his congenial atmosphere, his over-loosened tongue was just able to articulate, indistinctly, "wo, wo. *who* you?"

Now, Miss Susan being entirely unacquainted with such afflictions as that under which the Militia Captain, from Georgia, was laboring, fled to "ma," with the announcement that, "something was the matter with the Captain,—he must have a fit, as he did so funny," and begged—"Do ma, send for the doctor, quick."

"Ma," choosing to examine the condition of the patient for herself before sending for the doctor, entered the parlor where the Captain had dropped back to distilling low-wines on John Heard's breeches in his former social relations with the flies. She accosted him as the daughter had done, with a "good morning, Captain," and receiving no answer, repeated her salutation in a louder and more awakening tone. Arousing from his somnolent condition, the Captain, as before, was able "to sight" the matron with great labor, when he delivered the following: "If any wo—wo—*woman* ru—ru—run gin me, she ru—ru—run gin *a snag.*" Now, Mrs. M. recoiling from the danger of running "gin" the ugly snag before her, sent for Mr. Morton, who coming, and understanding at a glance, the ailment under which the Captain was suffering, packed him off in the barouche in which he came, re-shipping him to General Heard for treatment.

On his arrival, Heard asked the Captain as to the success of his adventure, when he informed the General that "the ladies, particularly Miss Susan and Mrs. Morton, were too intrusive, and that Mr. Morton made too free use of liquor about his house, for a gentleman of his temperate habits."

I met the cast-off Captain, some years after, in the mountains of Northeast Georgia, when his threadbare condition—being clad in the cast-off riggins of Billy Barlow—was very suggestive of his name, and the avidity with which he accepted an invitation to drink, significant of his protracted thirst.

The most telling and effective speech I ever heard, was delivered by an old Constable of Wilkes county, Georgia.

Old Peter Bennett wore a pair of shaggy eyebrows over a pair of black, knowing eyes; a pair of drab leggins over a pair of small legs; carried a pair of saddle-bags, filled with executions, beginning from the time of the massacre of St. Domingo,* on the left of a pair of long arms; wore a pair of coarse shoes on a pair of pigeon-toed feet, on which the owner stood with a firmness indicating he had unbounded confidence in old Peter Bennett, Constable of the French Store District, Wilkes county, Georgia. He was what is called "a high Jack Straw of an old fellow, that did'nt care a d—n."

Peter had been sued on a medical bill by a young doctor, as remarkable for his "assumacy" and pretensions as Peter was for unpretending, straight-forward simplicity.

Peter had been about Justice's Courts as Constable, and the Superior Courts as Bailiff of the Grand Juries so long, that he was as much at home in the court-house as a lawyer.

When his case came on for trial, he annoyed his lawyer so much with suggestions, that he proposed to Peter to argue his own case, to which the latter consented promptly, though his counsel was the most eloquent in the circuit.

With the ease and confidence of a practiced speaker, he told the jury, that "we planters must take care of ourselves." We have the power if we will stick together agin' those men who make their livin' by larnin'; now, you stand by me here, and when I am on the jury I will stand by you—let 'em prove what they may—if one of 'em should sue you—that is the way to do, and then, with all their larnin' they can't git the advantage over us. I know'd the Judge and Tom, (the first name of the plaintiff's lawyer,) when they were babies, and in their childhood, when their mammys slapped them about like puppies in the way—very good Judge, very good man, and I like him; so I do Tom, always vote for him—mighty smart man—but gentlemen, they git their livin' by larnin', and it's natur they should care most for men who git their livin' by larnin', and it's natur for we, poor farmers, to care for one another, too. I tell you, we must take care of ourselves, or they'll git all we have, so they will, and you know it; now stand by me, and I'll pay you off when in my fix. Why, there's Dr. Pope—mighty good Doctor, and good man, but he too, gits *his*

---

* The French store was established by refugees from that massacre soon after its occurrence.

livin' by his larnin'. He swore the charges was reasonable and usual—dollar a mile. Why gentlemen, I have rid all day in the rain, on my old gray mare, constablin', for less than that—that I have, gentlemen, and Dr. Pope says it is fair and reasonable, but you know it is onreasonable, and you are a gwine to say so in your verdict, I know, for I would say it for you. And then, he done my old ooman no good, for he put something on her sore leg, and it sizzed, and it fried, and it smoked, and it burnt, and it stunk, and she kicked·and screamed, and tore it off like she would go ravin' distracted. I onc't hearn of a doctor, when he got a case beyond his skill, gave his patients fits, bekase he was h—ll on fits. Well, now, I suppose he didn't know what to do with the sore leg, and he tried to make a burn of it, bekase he's h—ll on burns, if not h—ll on burns, he can make a hell of a burn. I don't believe he is no doctor nohow. (Here the plaintiff drew out a parchment, supposed to be his degree.) Oh, you may put it up, no body knows how you got it; you may have stole it, or you may have squirted about Charleston or Philadelphia, or wherever you went, and not minded your books, and paid your money for it, without knowin' anything. I am told it is all writ in some outlandish, that we unlarnt men can't know what's in it, some Injun, I suppose, for I've hearn it called Creek and Latin. Now, the Latin Injuns I know nothing about, but I do about the Creek Injuns, for I've been among 'um a heap, and they have their conjurin' root doctors—medicine men, they call 'um—but they can't cure no body, no more than the plaintiff. (Here the doctor said,)

"Ask my patients!"

"Ax your patients! they are all dead and four to six feet in the ground. Where's Billy Slaton's Sam? and Charley Gresham's Tom? and Truitt's Sukey, and a hundred others? Where is Becky Ogletree and Mary Thompson, and Billy Branen, and Joe Hampton, and all of 'um? It will take Gabriel's trumpet to call them, and they will be called in a higher court than this, when you'll be made to smell brimstone, and where your larnin' will do you no good, nor I don't know if you have enough to hurt you here, tho' it hurt my old woman mighty bad, but this jury ain't a gwine to let it hurt old Peter Bennett." And they did not let it hurt old Peter Bennett of "the French Store District, Wilkes county, Georgia."

CHAPTER V.

The Middle Circuit.—Leading Lawyers—Ned Bacon—The staunch old Methodist and Rebel Preacher—The young Convict.

What I have written relates to the Northern Circuit of Georgia, in which I have resided; but practising at one time in one county of the Middle Circuit, I cannot let it pass without saying it was remarkable for the courtesy and high breeding of the leading members of its Bar, who always give tone to the rest of the profession and indeed, I may say, in some degree, to the best citizens of the circuit in which they practice. These gentlemen bore themselves towards each other, in the court-house, with the same deference and urbanity they practiced in the drawing-room. Compared to the ill-nature and vulgarity—not to say brutality—I have noticed in some circuits, generally due to one or more leading members of the profession—it was the difference between civilized and savage warfare. For in one as well as the other, Christian and humane men will inflict as little pain and expense on their adversaries as may be compatible with the great aim and end of the contest.

There was the courteous and winning Walker, a born and bred gentleman; the lofty and high-toned Flournoy; the handsome, neat and well dressed Reid—just short of dandyism; the kindhearted and sunny Longstreet, and the courtly Wilde—immortalized by "My life is like a summer rose"—with his marked, intellectual face; the imaginative and benevolent Carey; the lamented Burnside, who fell in a duel; the restless, impetuous political leader, Glasscock, and the stern and honest Holt. They were all fine-looking and talented men, of the first order in the State.

I had often heard the older members of the profession speak in raptures of "Ned Bacon"—the "Ned Brace," of the Georgia Scenes—of his wit, his anecdotes, his personal appearance, his talents and above all, his divine singing.

At the period of which I now write, he came from South Carolina, across the Savannah river to Columbia county, in the Middle Circuit, to defend Dr. Walsh, who was indicted for murder. Old as he was he was fine-looking and manifested, occasionally, that the wit which had so often "set the table in a roar," was not extinct. I thought, however, that he barely sustained his reputation for eloquence.

Judge Dooley, as before indicated, was a little jealous of the

Augusta gentlemen, yet paid them the compliment of saying that if he had a son to educate and accomplish, he would, after his college course and tour of Europe, make him ride the Middle Circuit.

They were the only lawyers whom I have ever known to approach the standard of professional courtesy mentioned by an English writer, who, speaking of two advocates of the English Bar, said: "Their daily professional opposition ripened into habits of personal intimacy and affection, for so finely were the minds and characters of these great advocates constituted, that each of them seemed to have a livelier sense of the qualities of his opponent than of his own.

In political opinions they were wholly at variance, nor were their habits of thought more nearly allied. . . . . But the natural refinement, breeding, and inate sense of justice, common to both of them, created a sympathy more powerful than all their differences."

But little occurred at this, the only court, at which I practiced, in this Circuit worth mentioning.

On the trial of a cause, a very staunch old Methodist was put on the stand to impeach the credit of one of his neighbors. And when the usual question was asked him, he replied, "he did not know anything in the world against his neighbor, except that he was a Baptist, and he would not deny it himself, and, but for that, he would believe him as soon as any man in the world."*

I remember some of the lawyers gave an account of an amusing case tried in Richmond county, of that Circuit, during the administration of Judge Walker, who was remarkable for his kindness and sympathy for those in distress.

It seems a young man who had lately come to Augusta was convicted of stealing a bolt of cloth. Having been in jail for some time, he came into court with matted-hair, a blanket over his shoulders and other studied appearances of squalor and suffering. After conviction, he asked permission to address the jury, and was told by the Judge, that the verdict having been rendered and recorded, nothing he could say or do could alter the record. But insisting, and the indulgent Judge giving consent, the young convict rose and delivered (no doubt prepared) a very eloquent speech. A large number of citizens of Augusta, and nearly all the jury, were

---

*An old rebel preacher, as stern in politics as the witness was in his religion, getting into "a weaving-way" in a sermon during the late war, in his fervor describing how the redeemed would flock to heaven, said, "some would come from the East, some from the West, some from the South, and—and—and—in God's great mercy, a few may steal in even from the North."

immigrants from Virginia, which the young man, no doubt, knew. He told the jury that he was a son of the Old Diminion; spoke of his aged parents living at the foot of a mountain, whose grey hairs, etc.; of the Poplar spring, the school-house and the innocent boy, with satchel in hand, etc., in a way that melted down the Virginians and the kind-hearted Judge. The penalty was whipping by the Sheriff in the market-place, and the Judge, in passing sentence, recommended the young convict to his mercy. The foreman of the jury, an old Virginian, turned out, and, among the children of the Old Commonwealth, collected a handsome sum of money to dress up and start the erring young brother, of the old State, on his way to the house of his father.

Great sympathy for the unfortunate young man having been created, and the Sheriff, Peter Donaldson, recollecting the Judge's recommendation, went through the mere form of whipping, without inflicting any pain; and that it might be with as little disgrace as possible, he took the whip from one of his slaves—his usual executioner—who was standing ready, with whip in hand, eager to perform his customary office, and laid the lash on lightly. Then came forward the foreman, with his hat half full of bills to the discharged convict, and delivering them, said, "take this from your sympathizing Virginia friends of Augusta, that you may dress yourself and start again in the world. Go with our blessing, and may you be a better and a happier man, notwithstaning your youthful indiscretion."

The punished convict taking the money under his blanket and pocketing it safely, said, "You may all go to h—ll, you d—d set of fools," and walking leisurely across the bridge, disappeared in South Carolina.

CHAPTER VI.

The Western Circuit.—Early discovery of Gold—Cheerful feelings in the Mountains—Sensations excited by viewing Mountain Scenery—Advantages of Middle Georgia from the falls of her great Rivers to the Mountains—The place of the United States Capitol—Most pleasant recollections of my professional life—Population of the newly discovered mines—Court scenes—Cynthia Hyde and Polly Heflin—A spooney wishes to play cards, and how he succeeds—Lewie, the fiddler, at the camp dances—He and a North Carolina "laddie" test their literary attainments—His misfortunes—Letter to Lewie—Col. Stamper—How he won a wife, and how he was transformed from a Singing-Master into a Lawyer and Militia Colonel—His speeches and other exploits—Judge Underwood—Visit to Rabun as a Lawyer—Tiger-Tail and War-Woman's Creeks—Judge "T." rides the Western Circuit—His originality—Sulphur and a clean shirt—Amusing charges by Judges—Visit to Rabun as a Judge—Serenaded—Tricks of a waggish Lawyer—What the Gap *was* and *will* be—Reasons why the social intercourse of Lawyers is easy and agreeable—Top Duck at last—Trouble of having a reputation to sustain—The Dog Rackett—Widows and Taverns—Judge Clayton and his Anecdotes—The applicant for admission to the Church—The Negro's Sermon—The Man who was reading "Riley's Narrative"—Organization of Rabun County, and the Boy with the Cotton Rag.

The next and only circuit I shall notice, is the Western, (so named because it was the most Western when organized,) but now more in the North-eastern than Western part of the State. So, of the Northern, for it lacks much of being in the most Northern part of the State now, whatever it may have been when named. As Judge Underwood said of a lawyer, though I may not have been of very extensive practice, I have been of very extensive riding, as will be seen.

Some forty years since, during the early discovery of gold in Georgia, and I may say, the first in the United States—I went to the gold region, in the mountains of the State, to attend to an important gold-mine case for a client, when I became so pleased with the scenery, climate, freshness of the country and people, that I continued to ride the circuit for several years, and until I went on the Bench, in 1834. I have never been in the mountains of this State, without resolving to live there before I died; the air, the scenery or water, or all combined, have given me an elastic, happy feeling that made "existence an absolute enjoyment." To be conscious of life in such air, sunshine and scenery, is near of kin, I apprehend, to the pleasant feeling enjoyed by association with the light-hearted society of Paris. Indeed, there is no portion of the United States—if of any country inhabited by the Anglo-Saxon race—having so fine a climate, for a constant residence the year round, as all that portion of Georgia above, and North of the falls of her great rivers. It is as far South as one can live, in the United States, this side of the Rockey Mountains, to be out of the region of sickness and insects. On account of their vastness and magnitude, one cannot look on a lofty range of mountains, without feeling some of the awe and elevation of soul that is akin to the sensations inspired by contemplating the vastness of eternity. Fine music—I know not why—inspires the same lofty sensations. Hence, I believe, when looking on the ocean, grand mountain scenery, the vastness of an extensive prarie, or listening to fine music, one is as near heaven, in this world, as on any other occasion. For the reasons just given, Atlanta is the proper place for a permanent location of the Capital of the United States. It is more central than Washington; indeed, now that the country is all linked with the railroads and telegraphs, all places are central enough. Every one would prefer travelling a thousand miles to spend a winter in such a climate, rather than remain anywhere North of the Blue Ridge during the same time. And no place in the United States is more healthy and pleasant during the summer. It is now larger than Washington was for many years after it was the capital; and before suitable buildings could be erected, would be larger than it now is or ever will be. Many Southern men have been unable to live in Washington in winter, and all Northern men could reside in Atlanta the year round, and some of their lives would be saved by dwelling there in winter. No combined advantages of any place, North of the Blue Ridge, can equal those of the climate and health of Atlanta alone.

The most pleasant recollections of my professional life are connected with this circuit. The excitement of this, the first discovery of gold—more so than subsequent ones—had collected an excitable and strange medley of people, not only from all parts of the United States, but from many parts of Europe. The Cherokee Indians were then, also, in close neighborhood, and adjoining the gold and frontier counties.

The immigration to the State of Georgia had, for many years, been mostly from the Carolinas, and had principally followed, very nearly, the latitude of the old residences of the immigrants; the piney-woods people of those States, moving to the piney-woods of Georgia, and the mountaineers to the mountains of the same State; so that the mountaineers of Georgia, having always been such, gave society a relish to one unaccustomed to its freshness. The attendance of women in large numbers, often equaling the men, on the courts, gave them an animated appearance. Families would come in wagons and carts, and bivouacing round the villages at night, their camp-fires gave them a cheerful aspect during court-week. They backed their wagons and carts on each side of the doors of the court-house, during the day, until they made almost as many streets of the vehicles as those made by houses; the women would sit and knit by their carts, as they sold apples, chestnuts, cider, cakes, etc., while some would visit neighboring traders, others the court-room, and the young people exercised the ancient and honorable calling of gallantry, all which gave it more the appearance of a fair than court-ground.

I recollect, on one occasion, Cynthia Hyde, a wiry and sinewy girl quite in her twenties, and perhaps thirties, was indicted for an assault and battery on Polly Heflin, in that part of the Cherokee country annexed to the county of Habersham, when the evidence proved, that the aforesaid Cynthia had knocked the aforesaid Polly down with a chunk of fire at a log-heap. While the trial was progressing, the defendant, in the standing crowd, back of the bar, worked herself among the bystanders, smacking her right fist in her left hand, and declaring, in an under and suppressed tone, that she was "little in body, but mighty big in spirit," that she was "as supple as a limber-jack, strong as a jack-screw, and savage as a wild-cat!"

The unsophisticated simplicity of the population, gave the people a charming freshness,, which will be illustrated by one or two anecdotes:

A greenhorn, some eighteen years old, had heard that court was a great place for gambling and winning money, then abundant for that region.

So, after practicing for some weeks in the mountains with "an old deck," he had "got his hand in," and came to court to push his fortunes. Seeing a group of lawyers on their way to dinner, and supposing them "flush," he went up, and accosting them—as he would have asked for a stray horse—wished to know, "if any one here wanted to play cards?"

"What?" asked Gen. Harden.

"Does anybody want to play cards? Three-up—seven-up, or most any game, so thar's money in it."

There chancing to be a regular "sportsman"—*alias* gambler—standing near, Gen. Harden called and told him, "here was a young man who wished to play cards, and he had no doubt, a gentleman of his politeness, would accommodate the amateur."

"O yes!" said Moore, and seizing him by the arm, marched down to that den of his, from which no money ever returned, except in the pockets of the gambler, and over the portals of which should have been written, "he who enters here, leaves cash behind when he returns." Bull-calf, finding he was roped, began to pull back, but Moore, determined to secure his prey, dragged the victim forward, and the last we heard, was the captor swearing, "as you wish to play cards with gentlemen, you shall play," etc.

On our return from dinner, I asked Moore, how he had succeeded? when he said that he had broken the new sportsman, who had started on a capital of a dollar and a-half.

With the first money made, by my profession, I bought a negro fiddler, named Lewis,---called Lewie, "for short"---a pupil of the celebrated fiddler Billy, mentioned in a former chapter. Lewie, I thought, and still think, played a better fiddle than any other musician in the world, though he did play nothing but "Old Virginny" reels and cotillions, Ole Bull and the rest of the "squeakers" to the contrary notwithstanding. And I think I have some right to judge, as I must have more music in me than most men, having been drinking it in for more than half a century from a Jew's harp to an Italian opera, and not one breath having come out of me in all that time.

Lewie was a fine looking young man, though as black as black could be, and was as proud of having a lawyer master as I of owning such a fiddler.

I had Lewie with me at Clarksville, at court, during the height of the gold season, where there was great competition among the billiard-tables, drinking and other rude saloons, when his accomplishment as a fiddler was found to be a great bait to "draw custom." In that competition he was much more sought for, on account of his professional talents, than his master, in the courthouse, for his. The consequence was that his pockets were full of quarters and his head of the fumes of drink, with which he was caressingly treated. He was a man of talents, and soon understood his importance and the high respect in which he was held on account of his broadcloth and accomplishments. The young men told many anecdotes of his address and doings, some few of which I recollect.

When playing at the camp-dances, at night, the dancers being rude and untutored in the terpsichorean art, Lewie had much trouble to make them execute the figures correctly; and not knowing their names, had to be very personal in identifying them, by addressing them as connected with dress or other personal peculiarity, thus: "The gentleman with the copperas-pants will turn the lady with the striped dress; the gentleman with patch breeches will dance to the lady with a hole in her stocking; the bow-legged gentleman turn the lady with a wart on her nose, etc., etc."

One day---so the report runs---as he was playing in a drinking-saloon, with his head thrown back---and a fine head it was, though covered with wool---a "North Carolina laddie" was present whose biography was given me by my friend, Col. Stamper---directly to be mentioned. It ran in this wise concerning his education—the most important part of all men's lives: Having gone to school a few months, at the age of about fifteen, he went, the next year, to an "old-field school," in North Carolina, one summer morning, with an old Webster's spelling book under his left arm and a crab-apple walking stick in his right hand, and addressing the pedagogue of the log cabin, said, "Good morning, Mr. School Master! I have come to go into the larning business with you this morning."

"Have you ever been to school before?"

"O, yes sir! I made this book squat last year, I tell you sir!"

"Well, where abouts in your book shall we begin this morning?"

"Well, sir, I believe I would like to take a blurt at baker, this morning, sir! S-i-d, side, e-r—cider; b-r-y, bry, a-r—brier; and so on, Mr. Schoolmaster!"

Now, this blurting young mountaineer of the spelling book, stood in his shirt sleeves before Lewie, as he played Miss Lucy Long, with his crab-apple in his right hand and his left thrust in his breeches pocket; his wool hat jauntily on one side; his suspenders crossed before as well as behind, bringing his striped cotton pants several inches above his bare-feet; rolling his tobacco cud from side to side, admiring, as well as envying, the happy state and condition of this well-dressed and proud-looking fiddler before him. Lewie stopping to tune his fiddle and rosin his bow, North Carolina said:

"I G—d, I believe you low-country niggers think you are as good as white folks!"

".O yes!" said Lewie, "my master is a lawyer, and learned me dictionary!"

This was challenging Crab-apple on his strong suit, his "larnin"—for he had run on that line ever since he went into that "business," on that fine summer morning, in the old North State. After disputing a short time, they agreed to test their literary attainments by betting a-half dollar who could say the biggest word. Lewie slapped down, on the corner of the table, his silver half, "like a gentleman." He of the short breeches, putting up "an old-time seven pence," a plug of tobacco, an eel-skin purse and an old jack-knife, matched Lewie's half, by his pile; and now, he of the old North State, being a white man, and very confident, took "the first go." Like the Connecticut school master, who took off his coat to spell Constantinople, he prepared himself, by throwing out his quid, raising his crab-apple six inches from the floor, placing his left foot some twelve inches in front of his right, as if he wished to take a running-start with his weighty-word, he brought down his crab-apple with a vim as he ejaculated, "metamia"---trying at Mesopotamia, which he had stumbled on somewhere---and then he took another quid from the pig-tail that he had staked, with an air of ease and confidence that said, "now let any low-country nigger beat that, if he can."

After receiving the enemy's fire of light artillery, Lewie, feeling confident of an easy victory, promptly let off his heavy metal with the crushing word "sumculution," and saying "give me the money here," raked the pile into his hat, rose, and dividing with the astounded vanquished, the pig-tail, and pocketing the silver, he magnanimously returned his knife and purse to Crab-apple, with the admonition "never to run agin' lawyer larnin' till he went to school more."

Lewie, afterwards, having displeased me, I, in a fit of anger, sold him, and his new master, on account of bad conduct, sent him to Mississippi. Repenting of my precipitancy, I afterwards enquired for, but could never find him. Not dispairing that he may be above ground, I hope the reader will, if he knows an old negro named Lewie, who can fiddle old Virginia reels better than any other who ever rosined a bow, read the following letter to him; for such a fiddler will, no doubt, be my old Lewie:

HAYWOOD, January 17th, 1870.

To my old Servant, Lewie, the Fiddler:

I wish you, Lewie, on receipt of this, to come back to the old place. If you will forgive me my anger, I will your fault, and we will live together and die at the old place.

Mine eyes are dim, as your body is bent with age. I am bald, as you are grey with years, but with the warmth of youth, I will grasp with a boney and wrinkled hand, a hard and withered hand of thine.

I have now no cast-off broadcloth for you to wear—for I am as seedy as seedy can be. My canals are choked, my cisterns are broken and my fountains are dry; my fences are rotten, my roofs are leaking, and my barns are empty—all! all! Lewie, emblemmatical of my waning years, wrecked fortunes, and desolate country. You shall take up your fiddle—violin they call it now, Lewie—and play me some of the old Virginia reels and old-time cotillions, and to keep up the illusion, shall call out the figures, Lewie, as in days "lang syne;" and closing my eyes, I will dream back the days and jocund beauties of half a century since, when, all gushing with enjoyment, to the tune of your fiddle, I galloped with them in their silken flounces, sparkling jewels and pendant curls, down Head's long ball-room. Oh, those were jolly days and jollier nights, Lewie, when I was master and you were man. Though you can have no more luxurious living, your old mistress will give you your place by the kitchen hearth, where, if you will share with me my poverty, I will divide with you my crust.

YOUR OLD MASTER.

No account of the Western Circuit could make any pretensions to completeness which should fail to notice Col. Stamper, who rose from a singing-master to be Colonel of Militia, and one of the most notorious lawyers of the circuit.

The best judge of the female heart of any man I ever knew, said the nearest way to reach it was through the ears, and particularly by a good singing voice.

Music of itself, is a powerful agent in the tender passion, but when combined with a musical voice, it is irresistable. Hence the many "misalliances" with music-masters, and the many matches made at the piano. But the "sol-fa-la" man has advantages far superior to those of the fasionable music-teacher or the beaux at the piano, for he can bring to his aid three, and sometimes four senses, in a way not at the command of the two last. Having his male scholars on benches to his left, and his females on the right, he moves with a stage-strut as he beats time, gracefully, from bench to bench, flourishing his red bandana, and showing to the best advantage his fine clothes, from boots to paper collar; his swinging watch-seals and bright breast-pin; his many finger-rings as he beats time with his hands, and his gold or brass watch, as he consults the time of day. Bending over a feminine scholar with his well brushed hair fragrant of cinnamon-oil or odorous bear's grease, he takes her fan and as he sings the notes from the same book, fans the kindling passion into a flame. For toilet purposes he carries, in the crown of his hat, a looking-glass, and in his pockets a comb or hair-brush, strong perfumery and a few shining paper collars for all emergencies.

When the widow Wadman, in the sentry box, attacked Uncle Toby's two extremities by one sense only, even the cool and steady old soldier's center was put in motion. How, then, can we hope poor little Becky's heart to remain quiet when attacked through three of these organs at the same time? and when she resumes her fan, by its trembling, you can see this little instrument of love is all in a flutter. And then, when his school adjourns, the man of melody can follow up his suit by riding home with his victim exhibiting his gallant steed, bespangled bridle, silver-plated stirrup-irons and other trappings to the greatest advantage; and in the twilight of summer evenings, pretending only to teach his scholar music, he insidiously melts her heart with love and psalmody.

Talk of waltzes, yellow covered novels, walks by moon-light, boarding in the same house, philopœnas or candy-pullings, the sol-fa-la man is more dangerous than all—more dangerous than even love-powders.

A hawk, soaring at his ease in the air, taking a view of a flock of pullets sunning on a fence rail, can, with no more ease, pluck the comliest than our "knight of the gamut," as he displays his winning ways before his class, can carry off the belle of the neighborhood from the bench of beauties before him.

Our tuneful hero, having accomplished himself in flats and sharps, and collected a store of singing-books, left the mountains of Buncombe to sing his way to glory and fortune. He warbled his way through South Carolina, leaving a tract as broad as that made by Sherman in his march to and from the sea, desolate with broken hearts and ledgers filled with accounts for red ribbons, calico and new bonnets. Crossing the Savannah with sol-fa-la on his tongue and song-book in hand, he invaded Georgia with the "concord of sweet sounds," and melodiously marched in triumph until he reached the flat woods of Elbert county; there, using the advantages peculiar to his occupation, as above described, he, one Sunday evening captured one of his scholars, the belle of the neighborhood, and placing her on his horse behind him, rode to a neighboring Justice, where they were married.

When he met his father-in-law for reconciliation, the latter asked about his circumstances, and received for reply, "I *have* no circumstances, and I escaped hanging by escaping from North Carolina. I left with the precipitancy of the Dutchman who, camping near the warm springs of Buncombe, went to fill his jug with water, and finding it hot ran back to his camp and said to his son, "Hans, hitch up and drive right off for life, for h—l is'nt half a mile from this spot!" My voice is my fortune—the deepest bass in all the old North State—I have won a wife by it and will support her with the same instrument, for I can blow a living out of my mouth in a new way. I shall abandon singing sol-fa-la (law,) and study the law;" (and here a deep sol-fa-la boiled up from the region of his waistband). And study the law he did, and came to Wilkes for admission.

I once heard Judge Underwood defending a client sued in Franklin court by one Major Payne, of Elbert, warn the jury "not to suppose because the plaintiff is called *Major* Payne, he is entitled to any consideration on that account, for I will inform you that in the military county of Elbert no man is born lower than Major."

Now, whether our hero was born with the title, stole it as he sang through South Carolina, or picked it up in Elbert, where such distinctions were then as plenty as dog fennel in June, I know not, but so it was, he was introduced to me as Major Stamper, of Elbert county, an applicant for admission to the bar. I had the honor of being one of the committee to examine the student and report whether he was ripe for conversion from a singing-master into a lawyer. Reporting with the other gentlemen of the committee his fitness for the change, he received a license accordingly.

Our Major was a good looking, rollicking young man, with a sunny temperament, always in a good humor, particularly with himself—infectiously happy, never sick nor sorry—though often drunk and always hard run; waggish, with a good mixture of wit, humor and buffoonery; with feelings in tune with the highest notes of the gamut—and withal not such a fool as might be supposed from some of his sayings and doings—and very popular, as well on account of his good nature as his amusing drolleries.

The Major's admission was soon after the cession by the Cherokee Indians, of that portion of their territory out of which Georgia had organized the new counties of Gwinnett, Hall, Habersham and Rabun, lying in the extreme Northeast corner of the State, whose population was mostly from the mountains of North and South Carolina, particularly from the former State.

Our young lawyer resolving, wisely, to cast his fortunes among a people whom he knew so well, I will give an account of his grand entree into the field of his future greatness, in the language of Green Smith, then a lawyer of the Western Judicial Circuit, to which the above new counties had been attached.

It is necessary to premise that the bride whom our young hero had won by sweet sounds, was the daughter of Col. Hamet, a highly respectable gentleman of his county. And also, that the Judge of the Western Circuit (Clayton,) had lately been writing some very able newspaper political communications over the signature of "Atticus," and which obtained for him, by his political enemies, the nickname which he had assumed as a *nom de pl ue.*

Said Mr. Smith: " On the Sunday morning, as I was preparing to leave home for Hall county Court, some one called at my gate and asked if I lived there, and, on being answered in the affirmative, a gentleman alighted from his horse, and coming in, asked ' if I was Mr. Smith, an attorney of the Western Circuit.' Upon saying I was, he introduced himself as Major Stamper, who had married Col. Hamet's daughter, of Elbert; said that he was a North Carolina laddie, lately admitted to the bar of Georgia, and designed locating in the Western Circuit; that he understood Hall court would sit on the morrow, and that he desired to attend it and show them what a North Carolina laddie could do. I told him I would be glad to serve a North Carolina laddie, and particularly one who had married the daughter of my friend Col. Hamet.

We arrived at Gainesville, the county seat of Hall, that evening, and found the Judge, with several members of the bar, seated in the piazza of the village tavern. Before any introduction of my North Carolina friend, some one happened to address Judge Clayton as Judge, when my laddie friend rushed at him, with extended hand, exclaiming, ' is this you, Atticus? give us your hand, old fellow, I am Major Stamper, from North Carolina. I have married Col. Hamet's daughter, of Elbert county, have been admitted to the bar, expect to settle in your circuit, and have come to this court to show them what a North Carolina laddie can do.' The Judge was glad to meet him as a member of his bar and son-in-law of his friend, Col. Hamet, of Elbert.

The first case called on the Criminal Docket, was an indictment for larceny. The evidence made a tolerably strong case against the defendant for stealing money. My new friend, the Major, addressed the jury on the part of the State, in this style:

"Gentlemen of the jury, the scoundrel has got the money---stole it---can see guilt in his face---got it certain---d—d thief, gentlemen." Here he was called to order, by an attorney, but he continued.

You see, " Atticus, they are afraid of the North Carolina laddie, from old Bumcombe. Afraid, Atticus, I will turn them all down."

Here the Judge told him it was out of order, and very improper to use profane language in court.

This "confugled" him---to use his own expression---and he stopped soon without any more very great extravagances.

He settled in Clarksville, and his popular manners soon making him a favorite with the voters, he was elected Col. of the Militia. A regimental muster, shortly after, coming on, and though he knew nothing of the duties of his office, he agreed to go on the field. Borrowing a large, fuzzy headed stallion, named Hickory

John, with a long tail which he writhed much like a snake tied by its head, our gallant Colonel started to the field. Hickory John having never witnessed military exercises before, went to the field squealing and twisting his long tail, while his rider frailed with a hickory stick. He would have been unable to get Hickory John within speaking distance had not one of the Captains, who had an old mare used to such sights, rode in advance, and had not two of the Sergeants seized the bridle, so that the Colonel could expend his whole strength in frailing.

At length, advancing within hearing distance, our Colonel, taking off his old bell-crowned beaver, addressed his regiment after the following manner:

"Men! look on your Colonel and weep. I know nothing of military tactics, but I can speechify equal to old Tom Cobb and the North Carolina laddies on the juries, believe in this laddie, and I am h—l on a sassararer," (*certiorari*). Here Hickory John, giving his tail a curling twist, squealed and reared.

"See men, his neck is clothed with thunder, but never fear, for his back is clothed with a thundering Colonel. If any one complains that I am not a good disciplinarian, I will turn him over to Dick Lewis (a noted fighter) to discipline him well by next muster." Here Hickory John snorted and shook his flour-barrel of a head.

"He smelleth the battle afar off; aint you glad it is far off, and don't you wish it was further off, men? And now if any man has arer red he can have the honor of lickering his Colonel."

This time he dropped his old bell-crowned beaver and Hickory John, in his restiveness, stepping one of his hind feet in it and through the crown, it became so attached that he began to kick, and finally sent it some twenty yards to the rear. Proceeding bareheaded, he said, "Men, this will be a first-rate parade-horse for this regiment, as he will be dangerous to the enemy on a retreat, an evolution we shall, no doubt, perform oftener than all others. There is one evolution which you all have been well exercised in, that we will now perform, called the buzzard evolution, which consists in going in open-ranks to the carcass—which is to be found at Bill Glen's grocery—to take up the unfinished drinking of the day previous, where you will be dismissed and disgraced —and Hickory John ditto—and further, this Colonel saith not."

Sometimes when he had a good North Carolina jury, he would pat them on the head during his speech and say: "We North Carolina laddies know what is right; we men of old Bumcombe will do justice between man and man."

Georgia then had what was called an Inferior Court, composed of five Justices, which was substantially a County Court. He has been known, when the Justices decided against him, to poll them in this manner:

"Is that your opinion Judge A.? and yours Judge B.?" and so on, through the whole court.

On one occasion he was arguing before the same court, and said, "this is the law, as sure as the Bible and Blackstone tell the truth. If I am wrong I cave, if not, this Court will have to cave —the whole Bench, yes the whole five of you tumble in."

Like Judge Dooley, there were many sayings and doings attributed to our Colonel, and more than his share. Only those before mentioned can I vouch for. The following I tell as told to me by those who should have known of their truth.

Addressing the jury in a murder case, in which our Colonel seems to have prepared a lofty beginning, he said: "The sun had gone down behind the cloud-capped Yonah (a mountain in full view of the court-house) into the ocean beyond—for I understand there is a big sea over behind it somewhere called the Pacific—had gone down, gentlemen of the jury, behind old Yonah, and darkness had covered the Narcooch valley at its foot, when, inflamed by fiery hate, and consumed by burning malice, Tom Humphrey came and plunged his knife into the entrails of Pete Crump, and he wilted and died. Wan't it, was'nt it, gentlemen of the jury; gentlemen of the jury, was'nt it, was'nt it confounded mean?"

Delivering a fourth of July speech, after the usual denunciations of the mother country and laudations of the United States, he led off in this style:

"Whose afeared? whose scared, though she does call herself mistress of the seas? for if she is mistress we will be masters. And, my fellow-citizens, by rights they are our seas anyhow, for if there had been no Mississippi they would have had no seas no how. And if we were to turn that river into the lakes or the big cave of Kentucky, we would leave her ships in a puddle-hole at the bottom, surrounded by fluttering fish, turtles, snakes and alligators." Great applause.

In fifty-one or two he took the stump as a Whig orator, when he met a Democratic speaker, from Athens, to discuss "the great issues of the day." (No one has ever heard of any "small issues of the day," in politics.)

Now, the Democratic orator, coming from the literary and wealthy town of Athens, was dressed as became a gentleman from such a place—from such a city, I should say, for there are neither towns nor villages now. And our Colonel, the Whig, coming from the back-woods, was dressed like a back-woodsman. The Democrat happening to speak of himself as one of the "wool-hat boys," his adversary replied to that part of his speech, after the following manner:

"The gentleman spoke of himself as one of the "wool-hat boys." Now, look at this picture and then look on that. Here I am with my short homespun-jacket, cotton-shirt, copperas-pants, red-shoes, tanned and made by my old friend, Dick Spooner, and there lies my wool-hat, made by my other neighbor, Tom Hasklet. And there sits your "wool-hat boy," with his broad-cloth coat, linen-shirt, white-vest, so fine that I don't know what to call it, cassimere-pants, shining, polished boots, and there lies his fine beaver, too stuck-up and proud to come near my old wool-hat."

Here the Democrat rose and said, "if I do wear fine clothes they are not paid for."

"Well! said our Colonel, that is good democracy, as far as it goes, but it will be much better never to pay, unless you can make a security-friend do it for you."

One does not know which most to admire, the readiness of the Democrat or the Whig.*

If the reader will look at the map of the United States, he will notice that the old North State is reaching over the head of her little neighbor, South Carolina, to kiss the Northeast corner of Georgia's cheek. Now, our Colonel, living in Northeast Georgia, took advantage of this loving contiguity to pass over and practice in his native State, and, as characteristic of him, more than of that staid old Commonwealth, it is material to say that, coming into Habersham Court one Monday morning, with marked appearances of debauchery, I asked after his health:

"Oh! cave, caved, caving, in all its variations—just from Macon Court, North Carolina—broke up in a row—six teacups full of brown sugar and whiskey,—the dose every morning before breakfast—left three lawyers on the floor, not dead, but dead drunk—three more in jail—the Sheriff and Clerk fighting, and the Judge trying to part them—Macon fine county. If they would banish bail-writs, Sheriffs and Constables, and make whiskey free, would like to go to it when I die."

It has been the observation of all, how our language has been

---

* I have heard this speech credited to my old friend, Nash, of Madison, and I think rightly, but as it was reported of, and is set down to our Colonel, I will let it stand, as he would have said it, or something better if possible.

I have often regretted that the best stories in the language were too offensive to delicacy for record. And there is almost as much danger of offending prejudices to record good political stories, but good things must not be lost for such illiberal considerations.

enriched, not only by the introduction of new words—as fandango and ranche, from the Spanish; amateur and connoisseur, from the French, and as stampede, from the herdsmen of Texas, but also by new applications of old ones. The latter process I once witnessed or rather participated in.

One morning, as I was about leaving home for a distant court in the Western Circuit, I met a political friend and professional brother coming from the post-office, delighted with some good news he had just received, and which he announced by saying that a political adversary of distinction had "caved," meaning that he had been beaten in an election or met with some other political discomfiture.

This new application of the word "cave," striking me for its aptitude or for some other reason, I happened to apply it in the court-room soon after I reached it, in hearing of our Colonel, who caught it up with the exclamation of, "yes, that is it, that's the word!" Being a lawyer of "extensive riding," and for several years a member of the Legislature, and withal, doing his share of talking, officially and professionally as well as socially, and delighted with the word "cave," he sought every opportunity to use it. The consequence was that it soon became so current in the State that it could take care of and propagate itself in adjoining States, and with such success that I saw it the other day in an English periodical, with quotation marks, and applied as my old friend Bunch had, the morning I met him coming from the post-office, forty years ago.

Another instance of how "great a fire a little matter kindleth" may be worth mentioning:

A school-master, named Butt J. Wagstaff, indicted in Lincoln county, gave bond for his appearance at court. Having failed to appear, in the process of forfeiture his name had to be called often. Its strangeness having struck a lawyer as forcibly as the application of cave had Stamper, and the former, during court, losing a case unexpectedly, "caved," and not knowing what better to do, in his confusion and mortification, told the Sheriff to call Butt J. Wagstaff. From this beginning, the lawyers began calling on Butt J. Wagstaff whenever they "caved." In the parlance of the ring, it was throwing up the sponge. The silly practice extended from Lincoln on the East boundary of the State, to the Chattahoochee on the West, a distance of some three hundred miles, until at a court on the Western extreme of the State, a caved lawyer had Butt J. Wagstaff called, when the fugitive from Lincoln answered, came into court and asked the defeated attorney what he wished with him; on which the latter "caved" worse than ever, but concluded as the spirit he had invoked had unexpectedly appeared, he would appeal to it for assistance, and proceeded to tell the astonished pedagogue how he had lost his case, and had him called to advise what should be done. The lawyer was as much confounded at knowing that Wagstaff was a real man, as the fugitive was curious to know how he had been found out in his hiding place, and why he should have been called on for such advice.

The next most notorious and interesting character of the Western Circuit—but for very different reasons from those of Stamper,—at that time, was my old and valued friend, W. H. Underwood, who had been Judge of that Circuit, and for a long life since, was a leading lawyer of the Georgia Bar. I found him at the bar when I was admitted, rugged in appearance as was his mind. He had an unlawyer-like look, stammered or rather spoke with difficulty, but he had that all-important element of a lawyer—an ability to see the strong points of a case, as well as a searching discrimination, which could always see the true difference between things not the same, however much alike they might appear to some.

He was then esteemed a humorist rather than a wit. Before he died he was an eloquent advocate, as well as a profound lawyer, and decidedly the greatest wit, of his day, in the State. The convictions of his conclusions, whether as lawyer or politician, were painfully intense, so much so that he was nearly his whole life on the weak side in the latter. He was led by his logic with a cord so strong that he was obliged to follow, let it lead where it might.

He not only grew in knowledge and eloquence, but in wit—which of all gifts is thought to be most independent on cultivation—so that in the latter years of his life he was even superior to Dooley in this captivating quality of the mind. He had a slow and distinct utterance of every word and syllable that gave a raciness to all he said.

Of many good things said by him I can recollect but few. The first and about the beginning of his reputation for wit, was at Oglethorpe Court, when the Solicitor and his immediate predecessor were disputing over that old bone of contention, the costs made by the latter and collected by the former, from fines imposed during his term. The incumbent, after a long and heated argument, closed by saying, "he was not very fastidious about it no how," when Underwood promptly replied:

"I now understand the derivation of that misunderstood word fas-tid-i-ous, which I now learn means, to hold fast and for a long 'te-di-ous' time."

Arguing with the usual fervor of his convictions, before a Judge reputed to have been very arbitrary, he was arrested, with Blackstone in hand, by his Honor, announcing that, "he decided against him and did not wish to hear any more law or argument."

Underwood answered: "By no means do I wish to read law with any expectation of convincing your Honor, but only to show what a great fool Blackstone was."

Preparatory to a scene between him and myself, it is material to say that, one of the pleasantest recollections of my professional life is our mutual friendship, which, I am proud to say, continued to the day of his death.

While I was Judge of the Superior Courts, passing through the town of Cassville one summer during a session of court there, I stopped at the village tavern for dinner, and rest of myself and horses. Walking to the court-yard to see some friends, the presiding Judge saw and sent his Sheriff for me. Going up on one end of the Bench—hardly waiting to give me the ordinary salutations—the Judge retired from the others, aying, "hold this court, I am tired, and must go out;" and go out he did, leaving me in possession. I had been there but a few moments when my old friend came and spoke to me. Putting his left foot on one of the steps of the Bench, and his left elbow on his left knee, he asked, "how long do you intend to hold this court?" I told him, "no longer than I could get away," and then telling how I got there, I said, "have your Sheriff and Constables ready to chase down a Judge, for I shall run too, the first chance I get."

Still with his elbow on his knee and shutting all the fingers on the left hand, except the fore digit, he placed the forefinger of his right hand across its fellow of the left and said, "do stay until I can make a motion, that will take but a few minutes, for we cannot make this Judge understand anything?" While uttering the latter clause of the last sentence, the right hand finger beat the left as if it was as angry with it as the owner was with "this Judge"—" and I know as good a lawyer as you, can have no difficulty about the matter."

After "soft-sawdering" me a little more, he went to his seat, and soon rose, and moved to dissolve the injunction. After arguing his motion at considerable length, and with his usual ability, he took his seat, when I stopped the opposing counsel, by saying, "never mind, Mr. Rockwell, the court don't wish to hear from you, the motion is overruled."

Soon my friend returned, and assuming the former attitude, with the left foot on the same step of the Bench—and the right fore-finger across and on top of the left as before, the former, beating its bottom fellow with much violence, as if it had been to blame for the failure of the motion—he said: "Well! you may go now as soon as you please, and I wish to God you had gone before."

Judge Underwood was counsel for the Cherokee Indians in their controversy with the United States, which lasted for several years. Nothing could have been more unpopular than his position, and nothing more admirable than his fidelity to his clients, and loyalty to his convictions of right.

At any place, at any time, nothing is more to be admired than the sternness of those who will stand up for what they believe the truth in defiance of the "*vox populi.*" The greater the majority, the greater the honor of braving its insanity, or wickedness. But at the time, and on the occasion of which I speak, there was a moral sublimity in the sternness of the man who could, even in the relation of attorney to client, prove loyal to the latter in such an hour, against the strongest and most sordid passions of our nature, that was an honor, not only to the loyalty of the profession, but to human nature. No attitude of the profession is so commanding. Nay, so sublime, as when, in defiance of an unreasonable and unreasoning multitude, the lawyer boldly faces the *vox populi*, or rather *vox diaboli*, in defence of his persecuted client, or of an honest, though unpopular principle—I have known unhonored heroes at the bar that would match any of the honored heroes of the field.

Gold had been discovered in the Cherokee country, in fabulous quantities, it was believed. The lands were to be lotteried off, and everybody, entitled to a draw, looked on the Indian attorney as one who delayed their possession of a fortune. He was in consequence, in danger of that lynch law, then being inaugurated to the great disgrace of the country.

The Indians refusing to sell their lands, Georgia had extended her laws over the whole of their territory, at which the indignation of Judge Underwood was lofty and in its furiousness, to some, amusing

Living near the Alabama line, he practiced in some of the courts of that State, and on one occasion, he was taunted by a young "squirt" of the profession, with, "not understanding what was law in Alabama, that the law of the gentleman from Georgia, might do for that State, but he would inform him that Georgia law was not in force in Alabama." Underwood, in reply, among other things, said: "My young friend has reminded me that I could not introduce Georgia law into his State, and, with much confidence, repeated the assertion. I think the young man is rather premature in his boastful congratulations, for I will let him understand, that, of which he seems to be ignorant, to wit: that

Georgia takes the liberty of extending her laws over all the adjacent savage tribes, and, what concerns the young man, personally, still more, with very little evidence or ceremony, she hangs or sends to the penitentiary, all the young savages that traduce her, or are in any manner, in her way."

At this time, Gen. Jackson was at the height of his popularity, and having taken strong measures for the removal of the Indians, was more popular in Georgia, perhaps, than in any other State; and for that reason, more unpopular with Judge Underwood than any other man in the United States, and he took every occasion to give his opinion of that distinguished individual.

To the astonishment of all his friends, he delivered a fourth of July oration at the court-house of his county-town, and some of them having expressed their surprise, that a gentleman of his age and distinction should occupy his time with such an insignificant matter, he gave as a reason, that he not only wished to abuse Gen. Jackson before a large audience but also by authority.

He, too, like Judge Dooley, had his controversies with his landlords at the taverns, but, unlike Dooley, all in a good-humored way. At a court, thinking his landlord was remiss, he asked John Mabry if he had taken the oath of the Special Bailiff.

"Why?" asked Mr. Mabry, the landlord.

Because you have "kept us without meat, drink or fire—candlelight and water, only excepted;" "and that is the oath which is administered to the Bailiff before he takes charge of the jury, John Mabry, and from the way you have kept us this court, I thought you must have taken it. If you have, John Mabry, I can certify you have scrupulously observed it."

He never forsook horseback and saddle-bags, while I knew him, for buggies or railroads, and always rode a fine animal, about which he felt great anxiety. Stopping all night with Charter Campbell, of Madison, when his bill was presented next morning, he said:

"Well! Mr. Campbell, do you really think I owe you three dollars for the entertainment of me and my grey-horse, Cherokee?"

"Oh! yes Judge! it is a fair and usual charge."

"Well! Mr. Campbell, if the poet had stopped with you, instead of saying, "man wants but little here below nor wants that little long," he might have said, " if man has but little here below, and stops with you, he will not have that little long."

During the Know-Nothing campaign, a drummer recommending his tavern, said, "It was a Know-Nothing house," when Judge U. replied:

"Well! if the landlord knows less than Jim Toney—his old landlord of the tavern—I shall not risk myself with him."

Having been asked the politics of a friend, whom he accused of fickleness, he said: " I can't say, for I have not seen him since dinner."

Judge Thomas, of Elbert—in which county Underwood once lived—meeting him, said the people of that county would like to see him there, and he (Thomas) thought he could make a pleasant visit to the old place.

"Yes," said Judge U., "there is an honest stupidity about the people of Elbert which is amusing, and which I rather like."

Some citizen of the county, who took the remark of Underwood as offensive, meeting him afterwards, rebukingly said, he ought to take it back. "Well, said the Judge, I will take part of it back, and since the county voted for Buchanan I will withdraw the word "honest."

As I before intimated, he was the most independent man in politics in the State, of his distinction.

Often, not caring for the red rose or white guelph nor ghibeline, he would thrust, right and left, his sharp cimeter into all who exposed themselves to his wit. However, in the latter part of his life he seemed to have settled down in opposition to Democracy as indicated by another anecdote.

Howell Cobb having made an appointment to speak at Lumpkin Court on Tuesday, for some cause, postponed it to the next day—the day for taking up the criminal docket according to the practice of the court. Underwood asking the reason of the postponement, and not receiving a satisfactory answer, said, "I think it a very proper time, as that is the day for taking up the Democratic docket, and if the defendants all should appear there will be a very general turnout of the party."

For a long time he was accused of being an old Federalist, of the Jno. Adam's school—which, in Georgia, then, was little short of a charge of theft, and having been taunted with it by a politician, who said, "there has always been but two parties in the country, and we class you with the Federalists, for all know that is your place." "Yes," said Underwood, "there have always been two parties, Federalists and fools, and I have never heard you accused of belonging to the Federalists."

On being importuned to move to the town of Marietta, he said he would not like to live there, but thought it the best place to die in that he knew of, and gave as the reason that he could leave it with fewer regrets than any other place in the world. And what may seem a strange coincidence, he died in Marietta.

Rabun county reaches round and joins North Carolina, as I said, over the head of South Carolina, "amidst rocks and mountains, and roaring floods." During one riding of the Western Circuit, I went with the lawyers to court in that county, to see the country, without any view to business, spending all my time during the day exploring the back-bone of the Blue Ridge. Hardly anything worth telling occurred, but such as it was, I will put it down.

Crossing the clear and rapid Tallula, some three miles above the falls, we went up the Tiger-tail Creek, so called because its beautiful and regular windings were like the motions of the tail of the tiger. As I ascended the mountains, my spirits more quickly boiled, as does water under like circumstances of increasing altitude, with pleasure, until I came to the little town of Clayton, which, like the ærie of the eagle, in the cleft of the rocks, is nestled in a gap of the Blue Ridge Mountains. (This remarkable gap is a depression in the Blue Ridge, where the waters of the Savannah, running into the Atlantic, meet those of the Tennessee, which, making their way into the Ohio and then the Mississippi, finally are discharged into the Gulf.

Here I heard a discussion about an action pending for a lot of land lying on "War-Woman's Creek," and upon enquiry I learned the creek was so named because a white woman, having been captured by Indians, was taken to its banks where they camped for the night, when the Indians falling into a deep sleep, she seized one of their tomahawks and buried it in the heads of her sleeping captors and then made her escape.

My next visit to this interesting part of Georgia, was to preside as Judge, to try the causes in which an official brother of the Circuit had been engaged as counsel. I had been preceded, at the last riding previous to my visit, by an excentric Judge, about whom many amusing things, most of which are forgotten, were told. He was a strong union man, and a New Englander, and when the nullifiers became so violent that some Northern men shrank from acknowledging their nativity, meeting one too firm to deny it, Judge Tracy greeted him heartily, because he was not ashamed of his birth-place, and said: "That is bold and honest. If you come from h—l bring a pocket full of brimstone with you." The old Jackson Democracy having failed to re-elect him, he said, in his abusive wrath, that "he was the first man who had ever brought a clean shirt into the party."

A case was tried before him in which one of the points was whether a stump of a knife, made by a country blacksmith, was a Bowie-knife, as set forth in the indictment, and the Judge being asked to charge the jury that it was not, said, "I charge you, gentlemen of the jury, that anything which rips g—ts is a knife within the meaning of the law."

It is pertinent to mention, in this place, that I once knew a very nice young doctor, called as a witness in a murder case, to describe a mortal wound in the abdomen, and using a great many technical words, not understood by the Judge, he became very impatient and said, "never mind, doctor, tell the jury that the accused cut the deceased in the g—ts, and they will understand you better."

Another Judge, after hearing, in an old case, a labored argument by several large and strong lawyers on each side, who spoke with much vehement gesticulation, opened his charge by saying: "Gentlemen of the jury, this is an old case, which has been roosting on this docket some five years, and has at length been argued with great physical ability, and if the law of the case could be mauled into you by main strength, it must have been by the severe hammering you have just suffered. From the volume of the pleadings, much ink must have been shed in preparation, and you are witnesses that much sweat has been shed in fighting this legal pitch-battle of Smith vs. Thompson."

One Georgia Judge said that the maxim that innocence was to be presumed until guilt was proven, had one exception, and that was when an Irishman was accused of an assault and battery or riot, for then guilt was to be presumed.

A lawyer addressing a jury, on a case proven by strong circumstantial evidence, repeated often that "ninety-nine guilty should escape rather than that one innocent man should suffer." The Judge, in charging the jury, told them, "the ninety-nine guilty had long since escaped."

Rabun being a very small county, far off and difficult of access, my predecessor refused to go to that court at the previous riding. Because of that neglect I thought it the more important I should hold it. Besides, I knew small counties were very jealous of their dignity and importance, and that remote ones saw and heard more during court-weeks, than all the year besides, and I determined to hold that court, though it was raining a storm and the road very bad. Reaching the Tallula river on Sunday evening, in the rain, I found that rapid stream too full to ford. I remained at a log cabin until morning, when two footmen coming by on their way to court, were put across in a canoe, and I gave them instructions to say to the Grand Jury not to leave until late, as I hoped the water would fall so I could reach the court-house before night; and also, to tell the Clerk, if I did not arrive, to adjourn for the two days allowed by law, as I would wait to the last hour, to cross and hold the court.

Borrowing a saddle, I crossed the river on one of my horses, and reached the court some two hours, only, behind the footmen, and notwithstanding all my pains and explicitness, there was almost a riot before I reached Clayton, the report being current that "one of those low country Judges had come again who swore he would not budge a step if he could not reach the court-house in his carriage."

Not long after my arrival my quarters were serenaded by one of Washington's drummers—who seem to be as plenty as his old body servants. I was told that he had always been in the habit of honoring the Judge with such attentions, and that on one occasion when a new Judge had been elected, a waggish lawyer told Mr. Williams, the drummer, that the new Judge wished, when he started to the court-house the first time, he should follow at about ten steps distance and beat the drum behind him all the way—which the drummer did with pride—accompanied by the usual retinue of boys, negroes and dogs.

I had often heard of a great battle fought at this celebrated gap, between a methodist circuit rider and a blacksmith who had constituted himself its defender against the passage of those pioneers, (the Circuit Riders) of Protestant Christianity; and for "the vindication of the truth of history," as Mr. Benton would have said, I inquired into the particulars, and would have recorded them in these reminiscences, for the benefit of posterity, did I not feel my inability to do justice to the account of the engagement as told me by a lawyer of the Western Circuit. Suffice it to say, after many triumphs of the blacksmith, a large burley brother, with a big hard fist, on which a walnut might have been cracked without extorting a grunt, was sent by his good Bishop as the champion of the Cross, who gave the victory over the sledge-hammer.

This notch in the Blue Ridge, which, at the time of which I write, was almost unknown, will soon be the great railroad crossing between the North and South sides of that grand old range of mountains, where stood the humble smithy will the earth shake with the ponderous labors of the rolling-mill and foundry, and the road along which the preacher rode with his Bible and hymn-book, shall long trains of cars, rising from tide-water, fly along with "the iron-horse" up here among the clouds, with thousands of tons of merchandise, from all parts of the world, for the dwellers on either side of this great back-bone of the United States.

It was during this part of my professional life that I had the good fortune to locate another well known incident of rude ecclesiastical history in Georgia.

I said, in the beginning of this chapter, that when the gold mines were first discovered, they brought together a most extraordinary collection of people from all parts of the world, and it may be added, they generated a sad state of morals. For the miners, working all the week in mud and gravel, would usually collect at a few temporary log huts, called a village, on Saturday evenings, where they spent their time, until Monday morning, drinking and gambling. A preacher in the interior or Georgia, hearing of this desecration of the Sabbath, took his stick and wallet—for he was too poor to own a horse—and went to one of these sinks of iniquity for the purpose of rebuking the sins of the place. Arriving at a little collection of mining hamlets on Sunday, about 10 o'clock in the morning, he found the whole population engaged at their favorite game of chuck-luck. He told them what he had come for, and began rebuking their sins, when they replied by jeers and sneers. Being a man of discernment and address, he soon saw who was the leading spirit, and managed to get his permission to preach at 12 o'clock, provided his sermon should not exceed half an hour in length. When the hour of twelve arrived, the leader—Jack Hanks—mounted the head of an empty rum hogshead and proclaimed: "Oh, yes! oh, yes! oh, yes, chuck-luck will be adjourned for half an hour to let the stranger preach!" And the stranger preached, Jack Hanks being one of the hearers. Of course the man of God dwelt on the sins of gaming and Sabbath-breaking. Finally he became much excited, and so much so that his audience, particularly Hanks, sympathized with him. In a very animated manner he described the situation of his audience, as between a mountain on the right, which they could not scale, and a river on the left they could not swim; and which converging, the two intersected a short distance ahead, in such a way that their progress would be arrested, and the devil being behind driving them forward, he asked, in a startling tone, "What will you do? what will you do?"

Jack, having become very much excited and absorbed at the preacher's vivid description, replied to the second interrogatory, "I shall splunge the river." A companion shaking his head as an admonition to silence, he replied "Need not shake your head, for not caring to face the devil, nor being able to climb that bare rock, but, as I am a great swimmer, I would splunge the river and risk swimming out."

I once heard a lady say to a gentleman, having some reputation as a wit, whom she had asked to a party at her house, "come now, Mr. H., give us some of your wit? Do, Mr. H., be witty?" Of course Mr. H. wilted, and his fountain of wit, however copious it might have been if left to its spontaneous flow, dried up. An anecdote told on request loses half the raciness of one given voluntarily and suggested by the occasion. So, people who assemble with notification expressed or implied that they are to enjoy themselves and contribute to each others pleasure, come with a task imposed, with an obligation that defeats the object designed, just as one who *tries* to appear easy in manner, will fail. Hence, when congenial people are thrown together by accident, without any task or obligation expressed or implied, or any character to sustain, they hardly ever fail of enjoyment.

Now, when lawyers are thrown together at the tavern, dinner-table, fire-side or in a piazza of summer evenings, where there are none of the responsibilities of host or restraints of guests, they meet under the most favorable circumstances for the pleasure to be derived from unrestrained conversation.

A pic-nic got up with pleasure aforethought is recommended because of its freedom from the restraints of a formal dinner party. But the party coming together with the pre-determination of enjoyment, and having others do likewise, come with their cup of pleasure diluted with the alloy of obligation. All the abandon of the pleasure-seekers is affected or under the suspicion of affectation.

In the days of Sulky travel, we took our cold dinners at the springs which in the mountain region of the Western Circuit, were abundant, and of that icy coldness so vividly remembered and longed for to cool the parched tongue of the fevered patient. In travelling from court to court, the parties were generally large enough for enjoyment; when the freedom of the pic-nic, at the dining spring was unrestrained, the wit spontaneous and the anecdote apt and appropriate. There was no host with responsibilities, nor guests with restraints, nor character or position to be sustained, nor promises of pleasure to be redeemed or disappointed. Each spoke when the spirit moved and said what the occasion prompted, drank when thirsty and of what he liked, having no waiter, thrusting refused dishes under his nose—to fight off. He eat when hungry, when he chose and how it suited him. Every one was his own guest and his own host, and enjoyment came unpromised and unbidden.

It was on one of these occasions that Charles—afterwards Judge —Dougherty, told in his inimitable way—not to be put on paper— of interviews he had lately had with two of his clients. One had been hard run all his life and his name often called in court, but always as defendant, and was usually very impatient of confinement to the court-room. It may be necessary to say, for the benefit of those not acquainted with the practice of the Georgia

Courts, the last business usually done in the Superior Courts, is the sounding of the Appearance Dockets, which consists in calling the new cases brought to that Term, A B vs. C D & C. Now, said Mr. D., I noticed my law persecuted client continued very patiently in the court-room during the last few days of the session, notwithstanding I had informed him his business did not require his further attendance. When the Appearance Docket was called at the end of the court, the secret of his diligent attendance was manifested. Listening with breathless attention until the Judge called a case, in which *he* was plaintiff, and giving his lawyer a nudge and triumphant wink he said, "top duck at last, I God, Charley, top duck at last!" and the little fellow tripped out of the court-house with the "stuck up" air of the sparrow when he said, "I killed Cock Robin with my bow and arrow, I killed Cock Robin!"

A man having a reputation or position to sustain, is under a very inconvenient responsibility, for to whom much is given, of him more is expected, and to whom little is given little should be expected.

If you have a reputation for wit, you are expected to keep the table in a roar, and blow jewels out of your mouth on every occasion; if for oratory, you are expected to electrify your hearers every time you open your mouth in public; if for candor, you are bound to insult your friends by telling them of the faults they have and have not; if for charity, you are expected to give "everything to everybody," as long as you have anything to give; if for firmness, you are expected to be obstinate, and if "convinced against your will" to be "of the same opinion still;" if for honesty, you are expected to let every scoundrel impose on you, lest he blow the breath of suspicion on your "unsullied reputation;" if for piety, you are expected to sit on a hard bench on a cold Sunday, hear some gourd-head preach for two hours, and say "mighty good sermon, mighty good sermon;" and if it be a reputation for bravery, you are expected to shoot or whip every one whom it is safe to shoot or whip. No man is "free, sovereign and independent" who has a reputation to sustain, whereas he who has none, travels through life without a load; he has nothing to lose but much to gain, for like naught, he is never in danger.

Though Mr. Dougherty's client (Hewet,) was not embarrassed with any of the troublesome commodity of which I have just spoken, his dog, Racket, had carried a heavier load of it than any of his canine brethren, since the dog in the manger was a puppy, to the day when the dog to whom a bad name had been given was hung. According to old Hewet's account, he had not only slain his thousands of his own race, but innumerable bears, wolves, panthers and wild-cats, and would have slain giants if there had been any in those days. The throwing of bulls and oxen for the butcher, was an agreeable pastime and light work for Racket.

Just as Racket's bubble reputation was on the crest of the wave, he was disgracefully whipped by Dandy Jack, a Showman's travelling monkey.

Mr. D. gave a very amusing account of the fight and defeat—that I am unable to transfer to paper — which showed how much the disgrace was aggravated, on account of Racket's reputation. He concluded, by saying, that Racket took refuge from all Dandy Jacks, under his master's bed, and the latter went to his lawyer to sue the victor for damages, when he was told by Mr. D., that Dandy, being a gentleman in insolvent circumstances, it would be fruitless, besides, if he held the vagabond to bail he would be unable to give surety and the costs would fall on the plaintiff.

I said in a former chapter, that the worst taverns were those in cotton countries, and I might have said, as I now say, the best in all parts of the State are kept by women. Women place more importance on household comforts than men. To a man the utmost extremity of destitution is to be "without a cent," to have "nary red." To a woman, it is to have "the very bed taken from under her"—not to have "the wrappings of her finger left." A man will first expend his surplus money on equipage, on his ground and the outside of his house; a woman on the inside, her table, furniture and all those elegancies and sweet little comforts that emphatically belong to home.

I have noticed that a house kept by the best of landlords, will be improved by his widow after his death.

Two of those sweet, neat little taverns, were kept by two widowed sisters, in the little village of Carnesville, in the Western Circuit. They might be filled like bee-hives and would be comfortable to the last. It was in one of these, by a bright fire, around which we had collected at night, that the witty repartee, the pointed and appropriate anecdote, and loud laughs of the free and unrestrained lawyers might be heard till late bed time. It was here that I first met the lawyers of that circuit on my way into it. And here I met Judge Clayton on my first visit to it, and the last time, I believe, he rode it as Judge or lawyer.

In chronological order, he should have been noticed before, but I cannot let him pass in silence, though I saw so little of him then and there. He was remarkable for his address, kind heart and agreeable manners. I knew but little of him as Judge or lawyer, but enough to say, that he could leave me in as good a temper with his decisions against, as the petulant and peevish Dooley, would, with his for me.

Judge Clayton was a wit, not much inferior to Dooley, and had more good anecdotes, which he told better than any one in the circuit, but they are nearly all lost, for want of a chronicler, but a few, which I will rescue from oblivion, for a short time, at least, by recording them in these reminiscences.

One frosty October night, by Mrs. Jones' large and cheerful fire, he told us of an application he once had to prosecute an offender for using profane language in a church. He said a man applied for admission as a member, and was required to give in his experience, which he commenced, by saying: "I was riding in the low-grounds one dark, rainy night, on a bob-tailed pony." Having the impediment of a hair-lip, and speaking low, a brother, of the church, asked if he would "speak louder, that he might be heard by all the brethren."

The applicant commenced in a loud voice, but when he reached the bob-tailed pony, it was as low as before; and a sister, asking that he would speak louder, that the sisters might hear what the Lord had done for him, he tried again, but when he arrived at the bob-tailed pony, his voice was weak as before. This time a negro, in the gallery, called out and hoped "the white brudder would speak loud enough for the black bredderen to hear what the Lord had done for his poor soul."

Neither the patience nor religion of the penitent could endure the torture any longer, and he replied to the "black brudder:"

"You go to h—ll, you d—d black scoundrel. Do you hear *that?*" and taking his hat walked out.

This led Judge Clayton to give us some others of the same character, the best of which cannot be recorded. He gave us an old negro preacher's sermon, parts of which I remember, such as, "My bredderen, the Lord put Adam and Eve in His garden, and tell um not to eat He nice May-apple, but Eve longed for it; now if she had wait till apple plenty, she might steal enuff, and de Lord would not make such a fuss about um. If you want to steal, don't take the fust tater, de fust green pea, de fust green corn, de fust fruit dat ripe nor de fust cotton open, but wait till dem plenty and den steal what you want, and de Lord won't make no fuss, if master does; but de master can't see in dark like de Lord, nor de Lord don't throw up every little ting to you like white folks does. Bredderen, de white folks say we aint fit for nothin' but nigers, not fit, even for overseer, but de Bible don't say so. It says: "One niger Demus, a *ruler* of de Jews, come to Jesus by night." Now, you know if he bin white he come in de day-time, but niger working in de day, could travel only in de night."

"I tell you bredderen, there be but two ways for sinners, one lead to hell and todder lead to damnation," (here an old runaway said: "well, I'll take de woods den").

"Ah! you go to de woods, de devil in de woods. He have great big eye like de pewter plate, long, keen tail like overseer's cow-hide, and his mouf smoke like a coal-kiln."

. . . . . .

Scripter say, "heap coals of fire on enemy's head," and bredderen heap um up, heap um up till you burn um all up. And de Lord command you to curtail de power of de devil, and bress de Lord, we will cut him tail smoove off, close to he rump."*

Judge C. lost his office by the most Judge-like act of his life. Georgia having extended her laws over the Cherokee Indians he decided the act unconstitutional, and just before the election for Judges was to come on, when knowing, as he must, that he could have done nothing more unpopular. And Governor Gilmer, very improperly, I think, charged the Judge with having been influenced by the distant relationship of Mrs. C. to Mr. Wirt, who was one of the attorneys for the Indians.

He organized Rabun county soon after its cession by the Cherokee Indians. When, on his first visit, he came within a few miles of Tallula River, he said, on arriving at the forks of the road, he asked the way of a man sitting under a tree in his yard, reading, who replied, that "he did not know, but believed the left went to the court-ground"—no court-house having been as yet built. He then asked where the right led to, the reader, without raising his eyes from his book, said, he believed "to the falls." The Judge then asked "how far to the falls?"

"Don't know, but think it is some three miles."

"How long have you lived here?"   "Three years!"

"Have you never been there?"

"No!" Eyes still rivited on his book.

"What is that you are reading?"

"Riley's narrative."

"And do you sit there reading those lies and not go to see one of the greatest falls in the world—one that others have travelled thousands of miles to see?"

The reader being too much absorbed with his "lies" to answer, —if he listened—turned over another leaf and read on.

---

* I doubt if good taste and proper reverence for sacred things will justify giving as much as I have of the black brother's sermon.

First the Judge left his sulky, with which he said he could climb a tree, then his horse and saddle, and took it a foot for the last few miles. On his way, the landlady of a cabin he had staid at, the night previous to his arrival at the court-ground, had, in a dingy cotton rag, wrapped him up some lunch, which, eating at a spring, a few miles from the end of his journey, he gave what he had left to a boy who had come to the spring for water.

When he reached the ground he found a shelter with a rude bench and chair for his use, as Judge, to administer the law, and rough poles with the ends nailed to trees, and stakes, enclosing a space of some ten feet square, for the bar.

While the Judge was in the midst of his charge to the grand jury the little urchin, of the spring, climbing on the bar-pole, and holding up the cotton-rag, aforesaid, called out, "here, Mr. Judge, is your rag!"

I said Judge Clayton's party—the old Troup and Crawford party—refused to re-elect him to the Bench on account of the most judge-like act of his life—an act as stern and lofty as the reply of Lord Coke, who, when importuned by James the first, to make a decision in favor of the crown, said, "I will do anything it is fitting an English Judge should do." In recompence for the wrong they nominated and elected him to Congress. Nullification was then beginning to violently agitate the country, under the name of State-rights—though many State-rights men denied being nullifiers. While in Congress, Judge C. became an advocate of the doctrine, and on his return a dinner was given him, as he came through South Carolina, in the year 1834, when he gave the celebrated toast—" He that dallies is a dastard; he that doubts is damned"—which seemed to electrify the whole South.

Soon after his return to Georgia a dinner was given him in Lexington, of Oglethorpe county, when he addressed the people, and I replied to him in my second political speech.

Judge C. had fine literary taste, and was considered the best writer in the State of his day.

I should not conclude this chapter without saying North-east Georgia has greatly altered since the time about which I have written, and will alter much more when the railroads, in contemplation, shall have penetrated that delightful and interesting region.

CHAPTER VII.

Miscellaneous.—Lawyer's Fees—Lawyer's Profits.

FEES.

The following letter explains itself:

"Enclosed you will find the Augusta Fee Bill, which I copy and send at your request. It is the same by which the Bar regulated charges before the war. Reference to it is somewhat neglected now-a-days, but we sometimes use it as a standard. You know in these times of poverty, we are compelled to be governed by circumstances of parties in making charges."

FEE BILL, *adopted by the Richmond Bar, July 2d,* 1852.

GENERAL PRACTICE.

Collecting sums under $100 with or without suit,	$ 5 00
Same by suit, rule or on mortgage, if litigated,	10 00
Collecting sums from $100 to $30,00,	5 pr ct.
Collecting sums over $3,000, 5 per cent on first $3,000 and 3 per cent on residue. The same commission to be charged in solvent cases, when the case is settled by the parties, or the execution or notes withdrawn from the Attorney's hands.	
Collecting over $100, and not exceeding $5,000, *if litigated*,	10 pr ct.
Excess over $5,000,	6 pr ct.
For each process, for bail, attachment or garnishment, in all cases, in addition to the ordinary process,	$ 5 00
For drawing or crossing interrogatories, or for acting as Commissioner,	5 00
For every oral opinion,	5 00
For " written do.	10 00
For drawing Deed of Trust or Lease,	10 00
For drawing other Deed, Mortgage, Bill of Sale, Bond or Power of Attorney,	5 00
For drawing Articles of Partnership,	15 00
For " Indenture of Apprenticeship,	10 00
For " General Assignment for benefit of Creditors,	25 00
For " Marriage Settlement,	15 00
For " A Will,	25 00

For foreclosing Mortgage of real estate, for any sum, in addition to the above collecting fee,	10 00
For foreclosing mortgage of personal property, for any sum, in addition to the above collecting fee,	5 00
For obtaining judgment in insolvent cases for sums of $200 and under,	5 00
For same for sums between $200 and $500,	10 00
For same for sums over $500—1 per cent on excess, and	10 00
For application for honest debtors or insolvent laws,	15 00
For same, if fraud be suggested,	30 00
For claim to real or personal estate, under $200,	10 00
For do do do do over $200	20 00
For retainer in cases under $300,	10 00
For do do over $300,	20 00
Cases in form ex contractio, not collection cases, when the amount does not exceed $200,	10 00
Same when amount exceeds $200,	20 00
Habeas Corpus,	10 00
Original bill in Equity,	50 00
Bill for discovery or injunction pendente lite,	30 00
Discovery at common law,	10 00
Bill or Petition for sale of trust property,	30 00
do change of Trustee,	20 00
Actions of ejectment, or for recovery of real estate,	20 00
Personal actions ex delicto,	20 00
Libel for divorce,	25 00
Motion for new trial, or in arrest of judgment and argument,	10 00
Drawing Certiorari and argument,	10 00
Application for Dower,	20 00
Mandamus or Prohibition,	25 00
Answering rule for contempt of Court,	5 00
For Commission of Lunacy,	20 00
For acting as arbitrator,	10 00
For preparing statutory leins,	5 00
For Possessory warrant,	10 00
For Distress warrant,	5 00
For writ for ousting tenant holding over,	10 00

SUPREME COURT PRACTICE.

For preparing case for Supreme Court,	$50 00
For arguing case in do	50 00

PRACTICE IN COURT OF ORDINARY.

Caveat in Court of Ordinary,	$25 00
Probate of Will and orders for letters testamentary,	10 00
Same if contested,	25 00
Petition and order for letters of administration and guardianship,	10 00
Same if contested,	20 00
Order for appointment of appraisers,	5 00
Preparing inventory and appraisement,	5 00
Petition and order for a year's support,	15 00
Same if contested,	25 00
Petition for order for sale of real estate and negroes, or either,	10 00
Same, for sale of perishable property,	5 00
Preparing annual return,	5 00
Petition and order for division of estate,	10 00
Same, if contested,	20 00
Preparing return of Commissioners to divide estate,	10 00
Preparing final return and petition and order for letters dismissory,	15 00
Same, if contested,	20 00
Petition and rule nisi for relief of sureties or revocation of letters,	10 00
Order absolute in such cases,	5 00
Same, if contested,	20 00
Petition and rule for execution of titles to real estate,	10 00
Order of Court expressing concurrence and directing titles to be made,	5 00
For each appeal to Superior Court,	20 00

CRIMINAL PRACTICE.

For drawing warrant in any Criminal case,	5 00
Appearing before examining officer in cases of misdemeanor,	10 00
Same, in cases of felony,	25 00
Appearing in cases of misdemeanor before Superior Court,	20 00
Same, in cases of felony,	50 00

☞ The above to be the minimum fees in all cases specified.

The above Fee Bill corresponds, nearly, with all the Fee Bills in the State, which I have seen. By the one for the Northern Circuit, adopted some half century since, no more than five per cent was charged for collections in any case, and it was reduced, according to amount, until it was no more than two and a half on large sums. Since the war many lawyers charge from eight to ten per cent for collections. Fees generally, I think, are larger than they were. forty or fifty years ago—with lawyers of reputations much larger.

PROFITS OF THE PROFESSION.

In 1852 I made a speech at the Agricultural Fair at Macon, and being pertinent to this miscellaneous chapter, I give from it an extract as follows—correcting one thing that time has since shown should be done:

"I have gone into one of the old counties in Georgia, where, probably, the lawyers, as a body, have been more prosperous than in a majority of the counties of the State. Within the last thirty-five years forty-five of the profession have been settled at the county court-house, two of whom have made fortunes worth from a hundred to a hundred and fifty thousand dollars; three, from twenty to fifty thousand dollars; nine have made from a scanty to a liberal support for their families; and a few, perhaps, increasing their property a trifle; seven may have supported themselves only; and twenty-four, being a majority of the whole, made less than a support for themselves. Some of the two last classes were men of fortune, independently of their profession, and like sensible men, abandoned a business "which would not pay." And some of the other classes, especially the first, had other quite important means besides their professional pursuits.

"The same town, during the same period, has had settled in it twenty-eight practicing physicians, who have succeeded, I have no doubt, quite as well if not better, than a majority of their brethren in Georgia; five of whom have made fortunes varying from twenty to fifty thousand dollars; eight, from a scanty to a liberal support for their families; the other fifteen, being a majority, have made less than a support to nothing. Some few of the latter class were men of property, able to live independently of professional aid.

"In the same town, and at the same time, there have been trading, one hundred and sixteen merchants and grocers. Seven of these, some with handsome capitals to begin with, made fortunes varying from thirty to one hundred and fifty thousand dollars; twelve, from ten to thirty thousand dollars; twenty-eight have averaged interest on capital, and fair wages for their labor, and the remaining sixty-nine were failures.

"In these statistics I have left wide margins, because of the impossibility of accurate information, though much labor and care have been spent, and I hope successfully, to approximate the truth—they are near enough to it, however, for my purpose."

The above was said eighteen years ago, since when death and the administration of estates have disclosed what was the fortunes of those esteemed then the most prosperous lawyers of the Circuit, of which the above is one of the ten counties composing it. And I feel safe in saying, the five named, as belonging to the first and second classes in said prosperous county, had made more property than any other five in the whole circuit. Indeed, the profession in that county have been unusually prosperous as compared with the bar of the State generally—so much so that the two most successful might be considered exceptions.

The above statistics refer to a time before the war, and when the profession was much more prosperous than now.

After taking the opinion of several gentlemen of the profession, I have no doubt that more lawyers in Georgia make under, than over one thousand dollars per annum. It is very unusual for a Georgia lawyer, without capital to begin with, to die worth one hundred thousand dollars, or even the half of it.

Entered according to Act of Congress, in the year 1870, by,
GARNETT ANDREWS,
In the Clerk's Office of the U. S. District Court for the Northern District of Georgia.

www.ingramcontent.com/pod-product-compliance
Lightning Source LLC
Chambersburg PA
CBHW020917090426
42736CB00008B/673